IN AND OUT
OF PORTLAND
WITH
CHILDREN

Third edition
Jane Petrlik Smolik

MidRun Press
90 Larch Row, Wenham, MA 01984
www.midrunpress.com

Third Edition

Library of Congress Control Number: 2006921059

Smolik, Jane Petrlik
        In and Out of Portland with Children/by Jane Smolik, 3rd ed. Includes indexes.

ISBN-13: 978-0-9664095-7-4
ISBN-10: 0-9664095-7-4

Cover Art by Teresa Flavin
Line drawings by Jane Smolik

10 9 8 7 6 5 4 3 2 1
Printed in the United States of America
Third Edition/First Printing

Acknowledgments

The author wishes to thank her mother, Florence Petrlik, for sharing her love and knowledge of the Portland area. She also wishes to thank her sister, Susan Hutchinson, for her invaluable editorial help.

Thanks also to her children, Libby and Taylor Smolik, and their cousins, Sam and Emily Hutchinson, Holly, Katie and Will Yermal, Jack and Ronan Cardus and Mary Jane Petrlik for their on-site research. And many thanks to her older children, Christopher and Adrienne for their creative input. As always, thanks to Randy for his encouragement and support.

MidRun Press and the author are not responsible for any errors or misrepresentations of fact in the listings of *In and Out of Portland with Children* nor for any injuries resulting from visiting any of the sites listed in this book.

Every effort has been made to ensure the accuracy of the information given in this book, but because price, phone numbers, and other facts change frequently, we urge you to call ahead before visiting any of the locations listed in this book

The purpose of this guide is to educate and entertain. The author and MidRun Press shall have neither liability nor responsibility to any person or entity with respect to any loss or damage caused, or alleged to be caused, directly or indirectly by the information contained in this book.

Remember all of Maine is area code 207.

CONTENTS

Dear Reader,

The idea for the first edition of this book came about one rainy Memorial Day weekend in 1997 when I had taken my two children to a local bookstore. Looking over shelves full of Maine guidebooks, I was amazed that there was nothing that specifically offered things to do with children. Surely with most of the population living in the southern half of the state and 9 million tourists visiting annually, this was a book waiting to be written.

I thought long and hard about what a good guide book should be. First, it should be big enough that you don't need to carry along a magnifying glass to read the print yet small enough to fit in a diaper bag, briefcase or purse. It should offer up things to do for both toddlers and teens and everyone in between. Out-of-towners should be directed to all the popular sites we locals have been going to for years, but natives should also be surprised by some of the findings and at how many places there are to visit with children.

Finally, while there is an *Index by Attraction*, I wanted to make it easy on the readers who find themselves in say, Gorham or Brunswick for the day. So there is also an *Index by Location*. Of course, many sites defied easy categorizing and could have easily appeared under two or more headings.

Portland, the state's largest city, is an exciting mix of hills, bays and islands. It is a lively city and with the influx of young, well-educated baby boomers the demand has grown for more children's activities.

You obviously agreed with me as we are now pleased to present the newly revised, updated third edition of our little guide.

All the recommended attractions, with the exception of those found in the *Excursions c*hapter are not more than a 90-minute drive from Portland under normal conditions. Check the *Distance From Portland Chart* opposite this page for the approximate mileage from Portland.

One word of caution: times, admission prices and locations of events change. Please call and check first before you head out with your family so that no one is disappointed.

In and Out of Portland with Children is meant to be referred to again and again. I wish you and your family happy "adventuring".

Sincerely,

Jane Petrlik Smolik

Jane Petrlik Smolik

p.s. Please let me know if there is a special place that your family has enjoyed and we'll try to include it in our next edition. Please write to me at: MidRun Press, 90 Larch Row, Wenham, MA 01984 or email: midrunpress@aol.com.

DISTANCE FROM PORTLAND CHART
APPROXIMATE MILES

Augusta	57	Sanford	34
Bangor	109	Sebago Lake Region	25
Bar Harbor	161	Waterville	78
Bath	36	Wells	30
Belfast	103	Wiscasset	50
Bethel	67	Yarmouth	10
Biddeford	16	York	41
Boothbay Harbor	59		
Boston, Mass.	110		
Bridgton	38		
Brunswick	26		
Camden	85		
Freeport	16		
Hartford, CT.	200		
Kennebunkport	29		
Kittery	50		
Lewiston/Auburn	34		
Livermore	50		
Naples/Casco	30		
New Gloucester	25		
New York City	320		
Ogunquit	35		
Old Orchard Beach	19		
Pemaquid	60		
Phippsburg	50		
Portsmouth, NH	50		
Rockland	81		
Rumford	75		

USEFUL PHONE NUMBERS, INFORMATION AND WEB SITES

Note: All of Maine is 207 area code

Time and Temperature: 775-4321

Greater Portland Weather and Marine Forecast:
688-3810 or www.erh.noaa.gov

Maine Turnpike Recorded Road Information:
1-800-675-7453 or www.maineturnpike.com

Convention & Visitors Bureau of Greater Portland:
245 Commercial Street, Portland   772-5800
The Portland Jetport Terminal   775-5809
www.visitportland.com

AAA: The Club's main headquarters are in Portland (775-5809) but there are branches in Brunswick, Kennebunk, Yarmouth, Auburn and Augusta.
www.aaa.com

Portland Press Herald: 791-6000
www.pressherald.com

Portland International Jetport
101 Westbrook Street, Portland
774-7301
www.portlandjetport.org

4

PARKING IN PORTLAND

Several shops and restaurants will stamp your parking ticket if you make a purchase in their establishment. Parking garages and lots that display the Park & Shop emblem will provide an hour of free parking for each stamp on your parking ticket. The METRO bus also accepts Park & Shop stamps for a free ride home.

Anthem Assoc. Garage 60 Spring Street
Casco Bay Garage 54 Commercial St. at Maine State Pier
Chestnut Street Garage Chestnut & Oxford St..
Cumberland County Courthouse Garage 188 Newbury St.
Custom House Square Garage 25 Pearl St.
DiMillo's Parking Lot Long Wharf/Commercial St.
Elm Street Garage 21 Elm Street
Fish Pier 350 Commercial (weekends only)
Fisherman's Wharf Commercial Street on Chandler's Wharf
Fore Street Garage 419 Fore St.
Free Street Lot 120 Free St.
Gateway Parking Garage 181 High St.
Harbor Plaza Garage 10 Union Street
Int'l Marine Terminal 468 Commercial St.
Midtown Parking Lot 44 Free St.
Monument Square Garage 346 Cumberland Avenue
One City Center Parking Garage Monument Square
Portland Public Market Garage Preble & Elm St.
Shipyard Brewery Fore Street
Spring St. Garage 45 Spring St/ Free Street
Temple Street Parking Garage 11 Temple & Middle St.
Top of the Old Port 119 Pearl St. & Congress St.

Getting Around

GETTING HERE IN THE FIRST PLACE

Air Travel: Portland International Jetport, 1001 Westbrook Street, Portland (207-774-7301) has regularly scheduled flights served by several airlines. www.porlandjetport.com.

Bus Lines: Concord Trailways (800-639-3317) or (207-829-1151) provides non-stop service to Boston, Logan Airport, and coastal Maine. They are located at the Portland Transportation Center which also houses the Amtrak Downeaster station. www.concordtrailways.com

Vermont Transit Lines (800-451-3292) or (207-772-6587) located at 950 Congress Street provides a Boston/Portland/Bangor/Bar Harbor loop. www.vermonttransit.com

By Auto: The Maine Turnpike, Rt. I-95, starts where the state begins in Kittery and ends in the state's capital, Augusta. For travel conditions on the turnpike, phone (800-675-PIKE). A more scenic route up the coast is Route 1, which for the most part parallels the turnpike. Be forewarned that weekend traffic on both routes is peak in the summer months. www.maineturnpike.com

Train: Amtrak/DOWNEASTER (800-USA-RAIL) is located in the modern Portland Transportation Center (207-828-1151). It provides four round trips daily between Portland and Boston's North Station with eight stops in between (see page 172).

ONCE YOU ARE HERE

Bus Service: Greater Portland Metro, (207-774-0351) provides local transportaion to hotels, shopping and attractions. One way is $1.00, exact fare. www.gpmetrobus.com

Portland Explorer, (207-772-4457) is an express bus service connecting Portland's Transportation Terminals, select hotels, the Maine Mall and the Old Port from May through October. www.gpcog.org

Down by the Sea

Like ships in an armada, the islands of Casco Bay seem to march into the deep harbor bejeweled with fir-tipped trees and granite bound ledges. They were originally inhabited by many Native Americans who summered on the islands to escape the heat, much as Portlanders do today. They were nicknamed the Calendar Islands because seventeenth-century explorer John Smith incorrectly thought there were 365 of them. You will read very authoritative accounts of the islands where people claim there are anywhere from 123 to 136 islands. Apparently the number you choose depends on the tides and how you define an island.

Founded in 1845, Casco Bay Lines is the oldest continuously operating ferry in the country and the lifeline to those islands that are inhabited year-round such as Peaks, Long, Great Diamond, Little Diamond, Great Chebeague and Cliff. These islands can also be visited year-round on the Casco Bay Lines regular mailboat. Biking is the perfect way to discover the islands, with Peaks being the closest to Portland. Since Cliff is the last stop CBL makes, you will have to wait a bit longer to get a ferry back to the mainland from there. The islands were of strategic importance during WW II, and abandoned gun emplacements and cement bunkers are still found. Children's imaginations are sparked for hours. That pirates and Indians also roamed here make the prospect of buried treasures and arrowheads a further enticement.

While biking around one of these islands ranks high on the list of things to do here, sailing or just cruising the harbor and coastline are also invigorating ways to enjoy the spectacular bounty of the state's southern coast. On both Peaks and Chebeague you can rent bikes once on the island.

CASCO BAY LINES
56 Commercial Street, Portland
207-774-7871 or www.cascobaylines.com

Known locally simply as CBL, this is the oldest continuous ferry service in America. It serves six islands in Casco Bay: Peaks, Little Diamond, Great Diamond, Long, Chebeague and Cliff. In the summer, they also offer a daily cruise to Bailey Island. Rates will vary, depending on where and when you are going.

There are 5-minute parking spaces alongside the terminal building for loading and unloading only. The two closest public parking lots are the Casco Bay Garage (207-761-9591) which is adjacent to CBL and the Portland Ocean Terminal (207-871-5816) located across from CBL (see also *Parking in Portland*).

Their Diamond Pass scenic cruise follows an inner bay route past Little Diamond, Great Diamond and Peaks Island and takes 1 hour and 45 minutes.

CBL accepts MasterCard or Visa and there is an ATM located in the terminal.

CHEBEAGUE TRANSPORTATION COMPANY
Cousins Island, Yarmouth
207-846-3700
www.chebeaguetrans.com

Chebeague Transportation Company offers service between Yarmouth and Chebeague Island. They operate two parking lots. The Route 1 satellite parking lot in Cumberland provides a shuttle bus or van that meets all scheduled ferry trips. The fee to park is $15 a day. The parking lot on Cousins Island in Yarmouth is available only to residents for overnight and weekend parking. Weekday parking is permitted on a space-available basis from 7 a.m. to 5 p.m. for a fee of $15 per day.

■ATLANTIC SEAL CRUISES
Town Wharf, South Freeport
207-865-6112
Open Memorial Day weekend-Sept. 30

Explore island trails and watch for seals on one of two daily Eagle Island Adventure cruises. Departures at 9:30 a.m. and 1:30 p.m. Return is three hours later. You'll watch a lobstering demonstration, except on Sunday, when it is prohibited by law. Eagle Island is the home of the late Admiral Peary and you'll spend about an hour visiting his residence. All cruises are narrated.

■BAILEY ISLAND

Harpswell

From Interstate 295 take exit 31 (Topsham). Get on Route 196, the coastal connector, and follow signs to Cook's Corner via Route 1. Take Route 24 south to Bailey Island, about 13 miles. Or take Casco Bay Lines (207-774-7871) Bailey Island Cruise, offered daily late June to Labor Day.
www.cascobaylines.com

If you take the CBL ferry, it will take 6 hours and cover the full length of Casco Bay. As the boat leaves Portland, it cruises past lighthouses and forts while the narrator explains the area's history . Other sights on this 40-mile, round-trip journey include lobstermen tending their traps and Admiral Peary's home on Eagle Island.

Be on the lookout for porpoises, bottlenose dolphins and, if you are lucky, pilot whales swimming alongside or near the boat. It can be chilly, so dress in layers.

But like Mackworth and Cousins Islands, Bailey is also accessible by bridge.

The island has two well-known seafood restaurants to choose from. Cook's Lobster House is close to the ferry pier. About a half mile from Cook's Wharf on Route 24, Estes is a simpler, less crowded, but equally delicious alternative.

The island is 2.4 miles long but barely a half-mile wide. The Giant Staircase is a natural rock formation that drops 200 feet in steps to the ocean and affords magnificent views. Tourists and locals both like to buy a bag lunch at the Giant Stairs Takeout on Washington Avenue and eat on the rocks or at the small park by the cove.

Land's End Gift Shop offers lots of little toys and souvenirs in a reasonable price range.

■BAY VIEW CRUISES
Fisherman's Wharf, 184 Commercial Street, Portland
207-761-0496
www.bayviewcruisesme.com
Open May-October

Enjoy a narrated bay or harbor cruise from the enclosed and heated cabin or on the upper deck.

A variety of different trips include a Harbor Lunch Time Cruise (12:10 to 12:50), Island/Sea Watch Cruise or an Attitude Adjustment Cruise (5:15 p.m. to 6:15 p.m.). Which is just about the hour that most children seem to need one! Have one of the local seafood markets package up a meal for you to take along.

A snack bar as well as a beverage center and restrooms are on board.

■CAPE NEDDICK LIGHTHOUSE
Nubble Road, York Beach
207-363-4422 or 800-639-2442
www.lighthouse.cc/capeneddick/index

Built in 1879, this popular landmark is locally known as Nubble Light. Looking out to sea from this vista, you will be rewarded with clear views of Boon Island Light and the Isles of Shoals.

The lighthouse and grounds are not open to the public, but Sohier Park, with its visitor's center, is only a few yards away and has a free parking area, restrooms and lighthouse information. Just down Rt. 1A on either side of Cape Neddick are Short Sands Beach and Long Sands Beach. Both are sandy beaches with bathhouses, lifeguards and parking that are open all year-round with metered parking in the summer. Short Sands Beach also features an amusement area and an Animal Forest Park where children can feed the animals in the summer months.

The Goldenrod Restaurant is located a few steps away at 2 Railroad Avenue. It is a York Beach landmark and home to the original saltwater taffy. Go in for lunch and the kids will be entertained watching the colorful candy being made.

If you just want a little treat, Brown's Ice Cream stand is also nearby and worth the trip.

During the Christmas season a small festival is held around the "lighting of Nubble Light" where it is set ablaze in thousands of holiday lights.

Some of the local boats offer cruises that head out off the coast to watch the big event from the sea.

■CLIFF ISLAND

Ferry service provided by Casco Bay Lines, Portland
207-774-7871
www.cascobaylines.com

Cliff Island is 8 miles and an hour and a half ferry ride from Portland but go and you will be rewarded by the serenity and turn-of-the-century character of this year-round community.

This is also the last stop on the CBL ferry so service here is not as frequent as it is to Peaks Island.

Consider bringing a mountain or all-terrain bike as there are four miles of mostly unpaved roads.

There are no public restrooms or public access to the waterfront but there is a sandwich shop near the ferry landing that is open in the summer. If you are looking to get away from the crowds and feel transported back into time, Cliff Island will not disappoint you.

■COAST WATCH & GUIDING LIGHT NAVIGATION
Long Wharf, Portland
207-774-6498
www.eagleislandtours.com
Open daily from May 21-October 31

Board either the Kristy K or Fish Hawk for one of several narrated tours. Spend a day on Eagle Island where you can visit the summer home of Admiral Robert Peary or opt for a shorter excursion on the 90-minute long, narrated Lighthouse Lover's Cruise.

■COUSINS ISLAND
Cousins Island Road, Yarmouth
207-846-2406
www.cousinsandlittlejohnislands.org

Like Mackworth Island in Falmouth, Cousins can be reached by driving over a causeway. As soon as you cross over the bridge, Sandy Point Beach will be to your left. There is a parking lot and porta-potties are available seasonally. You can either take the stairs or foot paths down the hill to the little beach.

To your right after crossing the bridge is a quiet four-acre wooded area known as Camp Soci that is a lovely spot for a picnic. There is a picnic pavilion and nature trails. Another bridge off of Cousins Island leads out further into the bay to Littlejohn Island. There is very little public access to the beach here as about half of the island is privately owned.

If your family still has some energy, continue on Cousins Island Road to the wharf where you can catch the ferry to Great Chebeague Island.

■DOWNEAST DUCK ADVENTURES
Commercial Street, Portland
207-774-3825
www.DuckAdventures.com
Operates from April-October, rain or shine
Reservations recommended
Tickets are available and tours depart from
Communiques, 163 Commercial Street

All aboard Portland's first duck boat for a 90-minute narrated ride/cruise. The 39-foot Super Duck runs according to the tides (it can only take off and return at higher tides). Tours originate in the Old Port and then splash into the ocean off the Eastern Promenade. The day we took the trip it was very calm and the boat plodded along at a gentle pace, keeping a lookout for any curious harbor seals.

After the tour, walk up Commercial Street and turn onto Moulton Street for a visit to Beals Ice Cream. The ice cream is all homemade and the shop is air-conditioned.

■EAST END BEACH
Eastern Promenade, Portland
Open dawn to dusk
Admission: Free

If you thought you had to leave the city proper to go for a swim at the beach, think again. East End is a public boat launch and a sand beach with parking for 70 cars. From the Eastern Prom, head down winding Cutter Street while enjoying the lovely view of the boats bobbing in the bay.

Fishing is prohibited but there are picnic tables, changing rooms and restrooms. There are park rangers walking about, though no lifeguards.

This is also the beginning of the 2.1 mile Eastern Prom Walking Trail that ends up on India Street.

■FINESTKIND SCENIC CRUISES
Perkins Cove, Ogunquit
207-646-5227
www.finestkindcruises.com
Open daily May through mid-October
Reservations recommended.

Finestkind has been conducting cruises of Ogunquit's scenic shoreline since 1956.

The Breakfast Cruise leaves around 9 a.m. daily, July 1 through Labor Day and travels for 1 ¼ hours out to the Island Ledges, a local habitat of harbor seals.

The Lobstering Trip (50 minutes) is a memorable way to experience lobstering firsthand. This is an especially good outing for kids. There are five trips every day except Sunday, when lobstering is prohibited by Maine law.

The Nubble Lighthouse Cruise (about 90 minutes) is a leisurely tour of the York's elegant homes and rocky coast. All cruises depart from the dock at Barnacle Billy's.

■FIRST/SECOND CHANCE WHALE WATCH
4 Western Avenue, Kennebunk
207-967-5507   or   800-767-2628
www.firstchancewhalewatch.com
Open Memorial Day to Columbus Day

First Chance guarantees sightings on their daily Whale Watch sail. This is a four-hour trip so little ones might be better suited to the Scenic Lobster Cruise aboard the Second Chance. Sailing out around Walkers Point, this trip lasts about 90 minutes and departs five times daily. All cruises are narrated.

■GREAT CHEBEAGUE ISLAND

Regular ferry service from Portland provided by Casco Bay Lines (207-774-7871) or from Cousins Island provided by Chebeague Transportation Co.(207-846-3700) in Yarmouth.

Five miles long and three miles wide, Great Chebeague is the largest island in Casco Bay. Over 400 years ago the island was the site of Indian feasts and, in fact, the name Chebeague is Indian for either "Cold Spring Water" or "Island of Many Springs".

The long and hilly ten-mile perimeter road is bounded by scenic vistas. On the northeast end, Hamilton Beach provides good swimming as does Rose's Point, located about halfway along the eastern shore. There is also a fine beach near the Casco Bay Ferry landing.

The island sports its own inn, several fine restaurants and three bed and breakfasts. Picnics can be purchased at the Island Market. Bike rentals are available. Boats leave Portland at 10 a.m. and return in the late afternoon.

■GREAT DIAMOND ISLAND

Regular ferry service from Portland provided by Casco Bay Lines. Note that there are two drop-off points on the island: get off at Diamond Cove.

Diamond Cove, originally Fort McKinley, has been turned into a year-round island community. Diamond's Edge Restaurant (reservations recommended) or the more casual Stowaway's Beach Bar and Grill are both excellent dining choices.

There is a small, pebbly beach that is nicely sheltered and a variety store for drinks and snacks.

Many of the island roads are dirt, not paved, so while bicycles aren't always practical, hiking or mountain biking would be a great way to enjoy Great Diamond.

■LONG ISLAND

Ferry service from Portland provided by Casco Bay Lines
207-774-7871

Lying between Peaks and Chebeague Islands, Long Island comprises almost 1,000 acres and is three miles long. A friend who knows these islands intimately says this is her favorite of all for biking. All the roads are paved.

The Indians were the first inhabitants, coming here to summer as soon as the ice had melted in the rivers. Now Long is the only island in the bay that is not part of Portland. The residents seceded on July 4, 1993, unhappy over taxes and feeling ignored by city services.

Quieter than the popular Peaks Island, Long boasts some of the most beautiful white, sandy beaches. Singing Beach, one of the prettiest, was named because when the wind moves over it just so, it sounds "strange musical notes of great beauty". South Beach, next to Shark Cove, on the back side of the island is also nice and sandy.

Lyrical names abound here the likes of Housewife's Sound or St. Mary-Star-of-the Sea Chapel.

A good meal can be had at The Spar Restaurant (207-766-3310) or you can buy drinks and snacks at the general store located near the ferry landing.

■LUCKY CATCH LOBSTERING
170 Commercial Street, Portland
207-233-2026
www.luckycatch.com

Climb aboard the 37-foot, Maine-built Lucky Catch lobster boat during the summer months. Most cruises consist of pulling traps while learning how these traps are hauled, set and baited. Pants and boots are available for the hands-on type.

Cruises run five times daily, Monday through Saturday, and last for about 90 minutes.

■MACKWORTH ISLAND FAIRY HOUSES
Andrews Avenue, Falmouth
From Route 295 in Portland, take Exit 9 North to Route 1 and cross the Martin's Point Bridge. Go right on to Andrews Road and follow the signs to Governor Baxter School for the Deaf.
www.fairyhouses.com

Inspired by Tracy Kane's award-winning children's book series *Fairy Houses* (Light Beams Publishing), the Maine State Conservation Department has designated Mackworth Island Community Village as "Fairy Houses Village". The official Fairy Village sign reads: "The village provides fairies with cottages during their visits to the island. We invite you to visit the village and admire the creativity of the builders. If you are so inclined, you may use your own imagination to expand the village or provide needed maintenance to the existing cottages. Thank you for treating the island with care and respect. This helps to keep the fairies coming back!"

Take along a bag so your child can collect special "building materials" as you walk along. There are a few specific Fairies' Rules:

1. Fairy Houses should look so natural they are almost hidden.

2. You should use only natural materials. Dry grasses, leaves, sticks, pebbles and pine cones are a few examples.

3. Be careful not to use or disturb any of nature's materials that are still living, especially flowers, ferns, mosses and lichen.

We would like to add just one note of caution: Remember the old saying, *Leaves of three, let them be.* Like any wooded area, poison ivy can be found on Mackworth Island.

A 1 ½ mile walking trail starts next to the parking lot and circles the island. Take a picnic and stop along the way at the small swimming beach or the playground. Near station number nine there is a path that leads to the late Governor Baxter's pet cemetery complete with markers for his thirteen beloved Irish setters and one horse.

■MARITIME PRODUCTIONS THEATRE CRUISES
Ocean Avenue, Kennebunkport
207-641-2313 or toll free: 877-933-0707
www.maritimeproductions.org
Open June-September

Cheers for this two-hour cruise featuring a costumed performance on the Maine Mysterious Rockbound Coast tour. Highlights include haunted lighthouses, shipwrecks, ghost ships, and women pirates. Weather permitting, they offer a 3:30 p.m. daily matinee and a 6:30 p.m. sunset theatre cruise. Reservations recommended.

■OLDE PORT MARINER FLEET
170 Commercial Street, Portland
207-699-2988
www.oldportmarinefleet.com

Want to try some salt-water fishing, but not sure the kids would last all day? Half-day harbor fishing is offered aboard the Indian II on Wednesdays and Thursdays throughout the summer. Choose between the 8 a.m. to 11:30 a.m. trip or the noon to 3:30 p.m. trip. Old Port Marine also offers full day whale watching cruises where they claim nearly 100% sightings on their trips. Whale watches leave at 10 a.m. and return around 4 p.m. Late May through June they run weekends only, but July and August have trips every day (weather permitting). During September and October they have cruises on Tuesdays and Thursdays. Remember to always bring a sweater or jacket even in the summer as the temperatures can drop quickly out at sea.

■PALAWAN SAILING
Long Wharf, Portland
207-773-2163
www.sailpalawan.us

Climb aboard a vintage 58-foot ocean racer and sail across

Casco Bay. Reservations are helpful. Palawan offers four two-hour long sails each day starting with a 10:30 a.m. morning sail.

■PEAKS ISLAND
Frequent ferry service from Portland provided by Casco Bay Lines

A fifteen-minute ferry ride will drop you off at this popular 780-acre island. Biking is the best way to tour Peaks' level terrain, so either bring your own or walk up Island Avenue and rent one at Brad's ReCycled Bike Shop (207-766-5631). From the middle of June through September someone is usually there. Otherwise, they use the honor system. They do have kids' bikes, helmets, baby carriers and some tandem models; and they will provide you with an island map. If you bring your own bike, Casco Bay Lines charges extra per bicycle.

As you tour the perimeter of the island you can take a swim at the beach located near the ferry landing, eat at one of the island's restaurants or browse through the Civil War Museum. The spot known as Norman's Woe is where the schooner *Helen Eliza* was dashed upon the rocks in a storm in 1869, inspiring Longfellow's famous poem, *The Wreck of the Hesperes.*

The sole survivor of the *Helen Eliza* wreck had also been the sole survivor of an earlier wreck in the West Indies and wisely decided to move inland to a farm in New Hampshire. Incredibly, one day he fell off a slippery log that crossed over a stream and drowned.

Jones Landing is located just off the ferry dock and serves food and drinks. More choices are available at Hannigan's IGA, Peaks Café, the Bakery on the Bay, The Peaks Island House and The CockEyed Gull. There's also an ice cream shop a block up from the ferry dock.

Note that the only public restrooms are located in the Community Building on Island Avenue about four blocks from the ferry landing.

■SAND BUILDING CONTESTS

★OLD ORCHARD BEACH ANNUAL
SANDCASTLE CONTEST
First Street, Ocean Park, Old Orchard Beach
207-934-2500 or 207-934-9068
www.oobmaine.com

Every July an amazing array of sand sculptures march across Old Orchard Beach (OOB). While the Annual Grand Masters Open competition gives us all something to aspire to, there are also amateur competitions. Participants are encouraged to buy an admission bracelet in advance, although they can also be purchased at the event.

Each year, the town hires a professional sand sculptor to build a 70-foot plus creation. In addition to the contest, live bands, beach games and a fireworks display keep this event lively.

Call to obtain a list of rules and a schedule.

★SAND BUILDING CONTEST
Ogunquit Beach, Ogunquit
207-646-3032
www.ogunquit.org

Admission is free to this family event. Registration begins at 8 a.m. and prizes are awarded in several categories.

Tips For Building With Sand

1. Sand must be damp to begin with. Keep a spray bottle handy in case your project starts to dry out.

2. Grainy sand holds together well but doesn't lend itself to finely carved details. The more clay-like the better, then it's good for sticking *and* carving.

3. Check the tides. You don't want to build a ravishing castle only to have the surf come and wash away your masterpiece too soon. If the tide is going out, it is best to build below the high tide mark so the sand is damp. If the tide is coming in, build at the high tide mark.

4. For the molds - use buckets, plastic cups, mixing bowls, margarine tubs, measuring spoons, cake, cookie and pastry molds. When using any mold or form, pack the sand down hard with your hands so it will hold together better.

5. Don't restrict yourself to ubiquitous castles. Try cartoon characters, pyramids, a computer, sphinx, a sleeping dog and his bone, a miniature town, mermaids, an octopus, a space shuttle, airplane, sundial and on and on.

■SEBASCO HARBOR PIRATE CRUISE

Sebasco Harbor Resort, Sebasco Estates
207-389-1161 or 800-225-3819
www.sebasco.com
Open May-October

Just 48 miles from Portland lies one of the finest inns on the Maine coast. Off their dock you board the 38-foot motor vessel, *Ruth,* for a 1 ½ hour Pirate Cruise. A costumed pirate is your guide as you land on an island and search for buried treasure. The mates are, of course, always successful and they each get a share of the reward.

Reservations recommended.

■THE WHALE WALL

Commercial Street, Portland

Pick up a fishing pole and head down to the Maine State Pier on the waterfront to see the giant 950-foot long Whale Wall. Painted by an artist named Wyland, it depicts the marine life in the Gulf of Maine. Stop along the way at one of the many fish shops to buy some bait and then toss your line in and wait for some unsuspecting mackerel or pollack. Occasionally you might catch a blue or a striper.

Located near the Gate 5 car ferry, it is well lit with lots of benches and even a picnic table. It is interesting to watch all the harbor's activity as the pier is adjacent to Casco Bay Lines.

A huge painted compass, designed by muralist Tony Taylor, covers the deck and points north.

OTHER CRUISE AND BOAT CHARTERS

Boothbay Whale Watch
60 Commercial Street, Boothbay Harbor
888-942-5363 or 207-633-3500
www.whaleme.com

Captain Fish's Scenic Nature Cruises
Boothbay Harbor
800-636-3244
www.mainewhales.com
Scenic tours and whale watching cruises

Deborah Ann
Perkin's Cove, Ogunquit
207-361-9501
Whale watching cruises

Devil's Den Charter
DiMillo's Marina, Portland
207-761-4466
Half and full day sport fishing trips

MORE SWIMMING BEACHES

Biddeford Pool, Biddeford
A wide tidal basin with beautiful sandy beaches and a gentle
surf. Sticker parking only, stickers available at Town Hall.
Parking is free after 5:00 p.m. Bathhouse. Lifeguards.

Camp Ellis Beach, Saco
Small beach where fishing off the rocks is popular.
Hourly parking available.

Drakes Island Beach, Wells
Limited parking in two parking lots.
Restrooms and lifeguards.

Ferry Beach, Scarborough
Route 207, Black Point Road
No lifeguards. Limited parking.

Ferry Beach State Park, Saco
Route 9, Ferry Road
Restrooms, bathhouse, play area, parking .

Fortunes Rocks Beach, Biddeford
Sticker parking only, stickers available at Town Hall
Restrooms and lifeguards.

Harbor Beach, York
Limited parking. Restrooms and lifeguards.

Higgins Beach, Scarborough
Just off Route 77
Limited parking. No restrooms. No lifeguards.

Kennebunk Beach, Kennebunkport
There are actually three beaches; Gooch's Beach is the largest
with soft sand and a gentle surf. Middle Beach is rocky;
Mother's Beach is sandy with gentle surf and a playground.
Lifeguards are on duty at Gooch's and Mother's Beach areas.
Gooch's Beach has public toilets. There are no snack bars.

Long Sands Beach, York
Metered parking at the beach.
Changing facilities and restrooms. Lifeguards.

Ogunquit Beach, Ogunquit
Accessible by trolley from several parking areas.
Restrooms and changing facilities. Lifeguards.

Old Orchard Beach, Old Orchard
Seven miles of white sand. Bathhouse, showers, parking
and lifeguards. The Portland area's most popular beach.

Pine Point Beach, Scarborough
Take Route 1 to Pine Point Road and follow to the end.
Snack bar, restrooms and parking.

Short Sands Beach, York
Parking and restrooms.

Willard Beach, South Portland
A nearly mile-long beach with views of Spring Point Lighthouse
and Fort Preble. Restrooms, lifeguards, parking for 75 cars, and
a snack bar.

Animals & Fish

■BIRDATHON
Maine Audubon Society, Gilsland Farm, Falmouth
207-781-2330
www.maineaudubon.org
Participation is free, but they encourage pledges

This popular annual spring event is organized in Falmouth but held at various locations. It draws both competitive and noncompetitive participants who try to identify as many bird species as possible within a single 24-hour period. Beginning "Backyard Birders" can have their own team or join one of Audubon's. Any geographic area may be covered within the state of Maine.

■BRUNSWICK FISHWAY VIEWING AREA
Hydro Plant, (off Route 201) Maine Street, Brunswick
Open May, June and July: Wednesday, Saturday & Sunday
Admission is free

Now owned and operated by Florida Power & Electric, this ladder was built so that migrating fish could swim upstream to spawn. There is a glass-walled viewing area and a guide to help you identify the kind of fish you might see. This area is only open at times when the fish are migrating.

If you are coming up from Portland, we suggest you combine this excursion with a trip to the Peary-MacMillan Arctic Museum located on the Bowdoin College campus and/or a relaxing swim and picnic at Thomas Point Beach (207-725-6009) located off Route 24 in Brunswick. Thomas Point Beach is open Memorial Day to Labor Day and offers a calm beach area with an adjacent playground.

■MAINE WILDLIFE PARK
56 Game Farm Road, Route 26, Gray
207-657-4977
www.state.me.us/ifw/education/wildlifepark
Open daily mid-April through Veteran's Day;
9:30 a.m. to 4:30 p.m.
Adults 61+ $4.00; ages 13-60 $5.00; ages 4-12 $3.25;
children under age 3 free

This Department of Inland Fisheries and Wildlife Game Farm is a great place to see all that is wild in Maine. Moose, black bear, fisher, mountain lions, lynx, wild turkeys and deer have all been brought here either because they were injured or abandoned.

A memorable excursion is the Owl Prowl where children learn what wildlife does at night under the light of the moon or bring your flashlight. Another popular event is the Halloween Night Hike held from 6:00 p.m. to 8:00 p.m. The Wildlife Chalk Art Contest for kids has a local artist giving kids instructions on creating wildlife art. Prizes are awarded. The cost for these events is the regular admission fee.

Round out your trip at the showfish pool/hatchery and the well-stocked Nature Store. Enjoy the interactive displays or relax in the picnic area before heading home.

The Park's picnic shelters and Outdoor Classroom may be reserved for parties and special occasions.

Directions from the Maine Turnpike: Take exit 63, turn right onto Route 115 and drive 1/10th mile into Gray Center. In Gray Center, turn left onto Route 26 North. The Park is 3.5 miles up on your right.

Tip: Bring quarters so you can purchase feed to give to the bears, deer and ground birds.

■MAINE STATE AQUARIUM
McKown Point Road, West Boothbay Harbor
207-633-9542
www.maine/gov/dmr/rm/aquarium/index.html
Open Memorial Day-September 30; daily 10 a.m. to 5 p.m.
Adults $5; ages 5 -18 and over 60 $3; ages 4 and under free

Operated by the Maine Department of Marine Resources, the Aquarium's exhibits were completed in 1995 and they have been a popular family attraction ever since. Boothbay Harbor is about an hour north of Portland so this is more than just a morning's diversion, but until Portland develops its own aquarium, it is this or Boston.

The main gallery resembles the rocky coast of Maine with regional fish and invertebrates hidden within the granite-like cliffs. There are interactive displays, touch tanks and a 850-gallon tank filled with sharks and skates that you can pet.

The aquarium is home to extraordinary lobsters of all sizes and colors including "Louie", who is nearly 17 pounds.

Presentations about Maine's fisheries and tours of the Department of Marine Resources Research Laboratory are also available. Visit their website to download a free Maine Coloring Book.

■OPEN FARM DAY
Various locations around the state
www.getrealmaine.com/visit/open_farm_day.html
Late July

Open Farm Day is held on a Sunday in late July. About 80 farms throughout Maine are open to the public for the day.

Within a short distance from Portland the following farms are usually open.

1. Avalon Farm
   1167 North Road, North Yarmouth

2. Keene's Painted Horse Farm
   404 Waterman Road, Buxton
   Miniature horse farm.

3. Sunrise Acres Farm
   42 Winn Road, Cumberland

4. Windy Hill Farm
   River Road, Windham
   207-892-2793
   Farm stand and a petting zoo.

5. Carter's Farm
   Route 26, Oxford (207-539-4848)
   Canoe and kayak rentals available.

6. Mountain Brook Farm
   219 Streaked Mountain Road, South Paris
   An alpaca farm

7. Stoneheart Farm
   285 Streaked Mountain Road, South Paris
   Visit Columbia sheep and watch a working
   border collie. Demonstrations of spinning
   and knitting from the sheep's fiber.

8. Neverdun Farm
   259 Log Cabin Road, Arundel
   A self-sufficient cooperative, they grow their
   own food and raise chickens, turkeys, pigs
   and cattle. Also, many solar collection devices.

9. Morris Farm Trust
   156 Gardiner Road (Route 27N), Wiscasset
   207-882-4080
   www.morrisfarm.org
   Open year-round
   Organic, non-profit educational farm that hosts
   educational programs throughout the year for
   children. Milk cows, bring a picnic and explore
   the trails, pond and waterfall on a self-guided
   tour. Wiscasset is about 55 miles from Portland.

10. Winters Gone Farm
    245 Alna Road, Wiscasset
    207-882-9191
    www.wintersgone.com
    Open daily 10 a.m to 6 p.m.
    *Meet the alpacas, and stroll the nature
    trails that circumvent the alpaca pastures.
    Gift shop sells items made from the animals
    fleece. Free informative video shown in the
    barn classroom.*

■PINELAND FARMS

Route 231 and Morse Road, New Gloucester
207-688-4539
www.pinelandfarms.org
Open year-round
Admission: Adults $5; seniors and children $2; under 6 free

Every Saturday Pineland opens their Valley Farm for exploration and activities. Families can view barnyard animals, milk a cow, and learn to spin wool into yarn. There are 25 kilometers of beautiful trails to hike in the summer and to cross-country ski in the winter. There is a General Store in the Visitor's Center, where all visitors must check in to purchase a trail pass.

Educational programs for all ages are available and guided farm tours are given every Saturday at 2:00 p.m.

Pineland is a great resource for families and is only about 30 minutes from Portland.

■THE GULF OF MAINE AQUARIUM
www.gma.org

This site is virtual only, since no actual aquarium exists at this time, but its website is loaded with information about The Gulf of Maine and a goldmine of information for anyone visiting or living in Maine. The sections titled *All About Lobsters, All About Turtles,* and *Marine Animals* are just a few of many that will interest kids. There are activity pages geared to learning about "creatures and places", facts and tales about things aquatic, such as sand dollars, lumpfish, loons and the winter beach.

■THE CENTER FOR WILDLIFE
Cape Neddick
207-361-1400
www.yorkcenterforwildlife.org
Not open for tours, except for their annual fall open house

The Center is a non-profit wildlife rehabilitation organization located on seven wooded acres near the summit of Mount Agamenticus. They treat over 1,500 injured or orphaned animals that are brought to them every year from throughout the region. The goal is to release them back into their natural habitat, but if they cannot survive on their own, they remain at the Center. Every September, they host an Open House where the animals can be visited. There are storytellers, raffles, a silent auction, and food. Go on line and join CFW's mailing list to receive an invitation to their next event.

■THORNCRAG BIRD SANCTUARY
Highland Spring Road and Montello Street, Lewiston
207-782-5238
www.avcnet.org/stanton/thorncrg.htm
Admission free

Here in Maine's second largest city you'll find New England's largest bird sanctuary. There are five short trails that pass through this 310-acre wildlife preserve. Visitors can walk the trails using their 32-page *Self-Guided Nature Trail.*

A Junior Naturalist Program for children in grades 3 through 5 meets several times a year. Sign up early though as there is usually a waiting list.

Directions: From the Maine Turnpike take exit 80 and head west on Route 196 (Lisbon Street). Turn right onto East Avenue. Turn right onto Sabattus Street. Then turn left onto Highland Spring Road at the stone pillar.

■THE CUMBERLAND FAIR
Cumberland Fairgrounds
207-829-4856
www.cumberlandfair.com

This family fair is always held the last week in September and features dozens of livestock exhibits, horse shows, and animal pulling events. The first Cumberland Fair was held in 1868 and this popular event draws thousands of visitors every year.

■WADE STATE FISH HATCHERY

Fish Hatchery Road, Casco
Village office: 207-627-4515

Maine depends on its hatcheries to support many of its excellent, well-stocked fishing areas. Opened in 1954, this hatchery was originally built to raise landlocked salmon. Kids can expect to see 2 to 3 lb. show fish, albino salmon and production salmon.

There is a hatchery and a rearing station here and it is the latter that is open to the public.

Casco is approximately 40 miles from Portland.

■WILDLIFE TRACKING: FAMILY PROGRAM
Gilsland Farm, Maine Audubon, Falmouth
207-781-2330
www.maineaudubon.org/explore/centers
Members: Adult $6; children $3
Nonmembers: Adult $8; children $4
Advance registration necessary

Come learn how to identify tracks and signs of animals you might see in your yard. The program starts inside as each child makes a plaster of Paris track of a deer, moose, racoon, or other animal, and finishes up with a nature walk, using what they have learned to find and identify tracks and other signs of wildlife on the sanctuary.

This is just one of dozens of terrific programs that Maine Audubon runs.

■WOLFE'S NECK FARM
Wolfe's Neck Road, Freeport
207-865-4469
www.wolfesneckfarm.org
Open year-round

Visit cows, pigs and sheep. Check out their special seasonal programs such as pumpkin hayrides and the spring calf watch.

■YORK'S WILD KINGDOM
ZOO & AMUSEMENT PARK
Rt. 1, York Beach
207-363-4911 or 207-363-3883
www.yorkzoo.com Visit their web site for discount coupons.
Open May through September
Zoo opens at 10:00 a.m.; Zoo Park and Games open at noon

Enter the Kingdom and get up close and personal with a white tiger, lion, zebra, elephant, llama, and even a kangaroo. Little ones love to get right in the pen with the small goats and hand feed them. They have elephant and pony rides, a bear display and a Wildlife Theater.

There is a separate amusement park where one of the most popular of the many rides is the *Jaguar*.

They also have paddle boats, a snack bar and gift shop.

From the Maine Turnpike take exit 7 (York's and Ogunquit). Turn left onto Route 1 north. The Park is 2 miles up on the right. You won't miss their 40-foot sign!

Crafty Kids

See also; Children's Museum of Maine, and Portland Museum of Art

■BEADIN PATH
15 Main Street, Freeport
207-865-4785
www.beadinpath.com
Open daily 10:00 a.m. to 6:00 p.m.

"Piles of sparkling crystals on strands, drippy Victorian beaded curtains, delicate drops of glass" - sound enticing? Come in and help your child pick out and string their own special treasure. Worktables, tools and friendly staff provided.

Pre-packaged kits for beginners on up make great gifts or stocking stuffers.

■CARAVAN BEADS & FIBERS
915 Forest Avenue, Portland
207-761-5947
www.caravanbeads.com
Open Monday 11:00 a.m to 5:00 p.m; Tues. 10:00 a.m to 8:00 p.m.; Wed. through Sat. 10:00 a.m. to 7:00 p.m.
Closed Sunday

No previous experience needed. Our kids all love to come here on a rainy day or when the have had enough sun.

The staff are very helpful and you get to chose your own beads from one of the largest selections in New England. They have in-store worktables and tools for your use.

They have added an extensive selection of yarn that includes many hand-dyed and specialty fibers.

Birthday parties are popular here as well.

■THE CLAY PLACE

670 Main Street, Route 1, Saco
207-286-2800
www.The-ClayPlace.com
Hours change with the seasons, call for their current schedule

A fun-paint-your-own pottery studio with lots of choices and helpful staff. They offer several children's art classes and weekly specials as well as holiday workshops for kids and a summer art camp.

A private event room can accommodate up to 25 people for birthday parties.

The "Read & Paint Program" is one hour long and is offered once a month. Staff read a children's book and then bring the story to life by painting pottery that relates to the story. Call ahead to sign up.

■CREATIVE CHILD ART
47 Black Brook Road, Gorham
207-839-3982
www.creativechildart.com

With the belief that every child is an artist, CCA introduces the arts to kids of all ages and abilities.

Projects range from simple two-dimensional drawings to more sculptural, three dimensional work. They hold evening classes for older children and after-school workshops for the younger artists.

Monthly Parent & Child classes allow parents to work along next to their child on an art project that is complete in one evening. Some examples of this include stepping stones, ceiling mobiles and collages.

They will gladly host a Creative Child Birthday Party. The summer camp is a popular offering where your child's imagination will be sparked from 9:00 a.m. to 2:00 p.m. The facilities are air-conditioned.

The calendar of upcoming events is always being updated so be sure to call or check their web site.

■CREATIVE RESOURCE CENTER
887 Brighton Avenue, Portland
207-797-9543
www.creativeresourcecenter.org
Open Tuesday through Saturday 11:00 a.m. to 5:00 p.m.
Closed Sunday and Monday

Established in 1975, the CRC has been doing something

good for the environment while at the same time showing a very good time to lots of kids.

This non-profit organization collects and sorts clean, safe, scrap materials from Maine industries then sells them at extremely reasonable prices back to you. After doing it so well for so long, it now serves as a prototype for centers in other states.

They have drawing paper, cardboard, wooden and clay beads, dowels, canvas, shoelaces and dozens of other unique materials.

In art/craft workshops children make flowers, butterfly pictures, ribbon windsocks, masks and puppets. But stop by and browse around anytime they are open. You'll be amazed at how imaginative your children will be. If they need a little coaxing, idea sheets and booklets are on hand for inspiration as well as kits to be assembled at home.

■GRAFFITI WALL

In front of Portland's East End Wastewater Plant on the Eastern Promenade Trail. The trail is accessible from the north end of Marginal Way or from the boat launch area on Cutter Street.

The city of Portland officials have designated this 180-foot long concrete wall as a legal spot for graffiti. The wall is open to anyone who wants to create graffiti. This community canvas has sported everything from talented and touching art (someone painted a beautiful American flag on September 11) to scratches and scrawls.

If you are driving down Interstate 295, the wall is visible from Tukey's Bridge.

■MAINE AUDUBON:
PRESCHOOL DISCOVERY PROGRAM
20 Gilsland Farm Road, Falmouth
207-781-2330
www.maineaudubon.org
Registration is required for all preschool programs.
One hour sessions: Members $63, nonmembers $94.50
90-minute sessions: Members $94.50, nonmembers $142

Maine Audubon offers several seven-week programs split up into small groups suitable for ages 2-3, ages 3-4 and ages 4-5. Sessions such as Buzzing Bees, Tadpoles, Good Night Nature and Curious Cubs last for an hour for ages 4 and under, and 90 minutes for ages 4-6.

The groups meet once a week for adventures into nature through stories, creative play, songs, art and hands-on learning.

This is just a small sampling of the terrific programs that Maine Audubon offers for kids of all ages. Their web site is very informative and you are bound to find at least one workshop or program to suit every child.

■MAINE COLLEGE OF ART
97 Spring Street, Portland
207-775-3052
www.meca.edu

Formerly the Portland School of Art, this four-year college's studio facility is located at 522 Congress Street. They offer a variety of Saturday classes broken up by age/grade. The Saturday School Classes are designed for grades 4-12. Classes for grades 7-12 include Creative Movie Making, Animation, Ceramics, Drawing, Oil Painting, Photography, Cartooning and Jewelry Metalsmithing.

Introduction to Knitting is open to students age 16 and older and lasts for 10 weeks. A one-day Boomerang Workshop is for ages 13 and older.

The Young Arts Programs, also held on Saturdays, are for children ages 6-12. Instructors are Maine College of Art students and projects vary from making a Life-Size Time Capsule to creating a Miniature Circus.

There are many classes offered so check them out online or call and request a brochure. Portland is fortunate to have an art college like Meca (as it's fondly called) reach out to the community with such rich and varied classes for our young people.

■MAINE MODEL WORKS
417 Route 1, Falmouth
207-781-8300 www.mainemodelworks.com
Open Monday-Saturday 10:00 a.m. to 5:00 p.m.
Sunday noon to 4:00 p.m.

This is a great shop that specializes in fine scale model railroading for the fine scale craftsman as well as the casual hobbyist. My 12-year old son found a half dozen kits that he *had* to have. They sell HO/N scale trains, parts, scenery and paints. New England railroads are their specialty.

■PORTLAND POTTERY
118 Washington Avenue, Portland
207-772-4334
www.portlandpottery.com

This combination gallery, school and supply store offers lots of regularly scheduled classes, workshops and even parties for young people in both clay and metalsmithing.

Over twenty different artists and teachers offer instruction to people of all ages and ability levels. The spacious studio is organized for wheel throwing, hand-building, kiln firing, metalsmithing, metal casting and studio rental.

Their supply store carries an extensive variety of clay, glazes and equipment.

■SOAP BOX DERBY OF MAINE

Information available from:
All-American Soap Box Derby Headquarters
P.O. Box 7225, Akron, OH 44306
303-733-8723
www.mainesoapboxderby.org

Experience the thrill of gravity. After being revived in 1995, the Soap Box Derby of Maine has soared in popularity.

Regional competitions are held at sites around the state as all Soap Box Derby competitions start at the local race level. The winner competes in the finals held each August at Derby Downs in Akron, Ohio and takes home a college scholarship.

Racers often try to find sponsors to defray the cost (about $450) of the kit required to build the box car. Racers compete in a stock class, super stock class and in a master's class. The web site will connect you to Derby races in Maine.

■SPIRAL ARTS, INC.

156 High Street, Portland
207-775-1474
www.spiralarts.org
Cost is typically a donation between $6 and $15 per session, depending on what you can afford. But you must register ahead of time. Classes are held in various locations.

Spiral Arts is a non-profit community arts organization that strives to make art affordable to all ages, through classes and workshops for adults and children.

Rev. Priscilla Dreyman founded Spiral Arts in 1992 and together with the board of directors came up with the name because, "We spiral around the city, bringing art to the people, " she said.

Recent classes have included a Knitting Circle, Clay Hand Building, Portrait Drawing and Bookmaking.

■START SCRAPPIN' AND STAMPIN'
226 Gorham Road, Scarborough
207-885-8660
www.startscrappinandstampin.com

The little storefront here is deceiving. You won't believe that they have two floors absolutely stuffed with every kind of stamp, paper, stencil and scrapbook paraphernalia known to man. They also offer workshops and classes for kids. Call or log on for their current schedule. Better yet, stop by and be inspired by the inventory.

Other Arts and Crafts Suppliers

A.C. Moore
200 Running Hill Road, South Portland
207-253-5178

Artist & Craftsman Supply
540 Deering Avenue, Portland
207-772-7272

Buttons & Things
24 Main Street, Freeport
207-865-4480

Craft-Mania Inc.
333 Clarks Pond Pkwy., South Portland
207-828-8033

The Craft Shop
597 Roosevelt Trail, Windham
207-892-0001

Michael's Arts & Crafts
490 Payne Road, Scarborough
207-883-8419

Ray & Robin's Hobby Center
734 Riverside, Portland
207-797-5196

Amusement Parks
& Arcades

■AQUABOGGAN WATER PARK
Route 1, 980 Portland Road, Saco
207-282-3112
www.aquaboggan.com
Open daily mid-June through Labor Day
10:00 a.m. to 6:00 p.m., weather permitting
Admission General Ticket (over 4 feet tall) $19.00;
junior ticket (under 4 feet tall) $15.00;
Toddler Ticket $5.00; senior ticket $10.00
Grand Prix Go Carts, Bumpin' Boats, Mini Golf $6.00 each
Water tubes can be purchased or rented at the park.

This is Maine's largest water park with five water slides, a wave pool, swimming pool, Water Wars, Aqua Saucer, Mini-Golf, Race Cars, Skid Cars, Bumpin' Boats and a Toddler Play Center. The park has gift shops and snack bars. Kimball Farm Homemade Ice Cream has set up shop and offers 40 fantastic flavors.

You'll find an arcade, spacious picnic area (no grills), locker rental and lounge chairs. Tired of being all wet? Try your hand at the beautifully landscaped 18-hole mini-golf.

Coupons are available on their web site.

Take the Maine Turnpike to exit 42. Follow Route 1 south for 4 miles. Aquaboggan is on the right.

■FUN-O-RAMA
13 Beach Street, York
207-363-4421
Open daily 10:00 a.m. to 11:00 p.m Memorial Day through
Labor Day; weekends only through Columbus Day

This large, indoor arcade caters to the summer crowd.

■FUNTOWN / SPLASHTOWN, U.S.A.
Route 1, 774 Portland Road, Saco
207-284-5139 or 800-878-2900
www.funtownusa.com
Funtown is open weekends 10 a.m. to 9 p.m. Weekends only
May until June 1. June to Labor Day, open daily.
Splashtown is open daily 10:00 a.m. to 6 p.m. daily June 1
through Labor Day (weather permitting)
Admission varies, but you can buy a walk around pass for $10
that lets you enter Funtown but not use the rides. Due to
limited space, you can only enter Splashtown's observation
deck unless you have purchased a Splashtown or combination
pass.

Billing themselves as New England's largest theme
amusement park, these "two parks in one" offer just about
everything for every age! There are major rides, kiddie rides,
water slides, eating plazas and even 18 holes of miniature
golf.

Grounds are landscaped and meticulously kept up,
making this an extra pleasurable stop.

Tip: Mondays are usually the least crowded days.

■JOKER'S FAMILY FUN'N GAMES
510 Warren Avenue, Portland (207-878-5800)
Route 1, Portsmouth, New Hampshire (603-481-7770)
www.jokersfunandgames.com
No admission charged

Family fun and games galore with over 150 arcade and video machines, indoor go-carts, a train and even a Ferris wheel. This 25,000 square foot, indoor amusement park is a wide open, climate controlled extravaganza.

A three-story, 55-foot long playhouse features spiral and speed slides, tunnels, rope ladders, foam forests and more. Adventure Falls Miniature Golf is available at the Portland location.

There is a rock-climbing wall and a 2,000 square foot dark room for Extreme Laser Tag. No wonder this spot garners first place when kids are asked where they most want to have their birthday party.

After everyone's worked up an appetite, a 52-item menu includes freshly made pizza, salads, hamburgers, sandwiches and salads.

■MAINE INDOOR KARTING
23 Washington Avenue, Scarborough
207-885-0058
www.maineindoorkarting.com

A high performance indoor karting course that is 1,200 feet long and 25 feet wide. While the facilities were designed specifically for adults, they offer a junior racing program to help train young drivers, ages 8 to 15, how to handle their junior-size karts. Juniors must complete a $25.00 Junior Licensing Class and be at least 50" tall. Classes are held every Saturday and Sunday at 11:00 a.m. Call ahead to reserve your child's place in the class. Classes are one and a half hours long and include on-track instruction followed by time trial competition. Each junior who successfully completes the training program will receive his or her MIK licence.

■OLD ORCHARD BEACH PIER
Off Rt. 1, Old Orchard Beach

Alternately known as the Coney Island of Maine or the Quebec Riviera because of its popularity with French Canadians, Old Orchard Beach is one of the most frequented beaches in the state come summer. But in a town where most stores have no heat, it is practically a ghost town in winter.

Located about 12 miles south of Portland, this Victorian era resort is famous for its 500-foot long pier filled with games, food and arcade-type attractions. When I was growing up the biggest treat of the summer was our annual excursion to OOB. Kids still love it.

Just a short walk off the pier you'll find New England's tallest Ferris wheel, the Galaxy Roller Coaster and Skee Ball arcades at Palace Playland.

■OXFORD PLAINS FUN PARK

888 Main Street, Oxford

207-539-8330

www.oxfordplains.com

Open throughout the summer 10:00 a.m. to 10:00 p.m;
weekends only spring and fall

Located across the street from the Oxford Plains Speedway,
the park features a Go-Kart Road Course, championship 18-
hole miniature golf course and a large video arcade.

In December the Park becomes Oxford Plains Snow
Tubing and is open Friday, Saturday and Sunday as well as
daily during school vacation weeks. Both hourly rates and all-
day passes are available.

Oxford is about 45 miles northwest of Portland.

■PALACE PLAYLAND

1 Old Orchard Street, Old Orchard Beach

207-934-2001

www.palaceplayland.com

Open weekends beginning in mid-April. Full-time season is
June through Labor Day, 7 days a week.

Admission free to enter the park

Unlimited Pass $23.95;

Kiddie Pass for children under 42" tall $16.95

Books of 20 or 50 tickets are also available.

Maine's premier beachfront amusement park is located on the
beach in the center of town. You can fly through the air on
two different roller coasters - the Galaxy Roller Coaster or the

family-friendly Orient Express. Or keep your feet on the ground at New England's largest pinball and video arcade.

Children twirl on a carousel of hand-carved horses one minute and soar into the air on a Pirate Ship the next. Let the kids test their driving skills against Mom and Dad on the Dodgem' Cars then cool off on the Liquid Lightning Water Slide.

In 2005, two new rides were added - the 40-foot EuroGlide and The Motor Cycle Jump. New England's largest Ferris wheel is located here.

For the younger set, Kiddie-Land offers over a dozen rides including Go-Gator, power boats, and Sheik Abdullah's Fun House.

You will find several food options, gift shops, old fashioned photos, palm readers and more. There are fireworks displays every Thursday night in the summer.

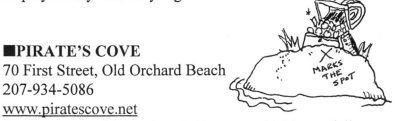

■PIRATE'S COVE
70 First Street, Old Orchard Beach
207-934-5086
www.piratescove.net
Open May to mid-October, 9:00 a.m. to 10:00 p.m daily

Two separate 18-hole golf courses wind around extravagant landscaping complete with waterfalls, mountain caves and footbridges. Each hole represents a different pirate theme.

■SEACOAST FUN PARK
940 Roosevelt Trail, Route 302, North Windham
207-892-5952
www.seacoastfunparks.com
Open daily, Memorial Day to Labor Day, 10:00 a.m. to
11:00 p.m.; Spring and fall, call for hours.
The Snowpark is open all winter.

Seacoast is a four-season family fun park located in the beautiful Lakes Region of southern Maine. In the summer, they offer mini-golf, go-karts, an arcade, bumper boats, skycoaster and picnic grounds. The brochure promises you will "drop like a rock and soar like an eagle" on the Screaming Eagle Skycoaster. The mini-golf course winds around streams, waterfalls and multi-level greens.

Come winter, pack up the kids and make a day of it with snow tubing, snowboarding or cross-country skiing. Don't despair if there is no snow in your backyard, Seacoast makes their own. Rentals are available. There is a lodge with a snack bar, and heated restrooms.

■VACATIONLAND
812 Route 1, Saco
207-284-7386 www.vacationlandbowling.com
Open year round.

Located only ¼ mile north of Funtown USA, Vacationland is a bowling and recreation center that features 32 air-conditioned lanes with full-color automatic scoring, as well as bumper bowling and glow parties for kids.

There is a billiard room with 9-foot regulation tables and a game room with a video arcade.

■VILLAGE PARK FAMILY ENTERTAINMENT CENTER
At the entrance to the OOB Pier, Old Orchard Beach
207-934-7666
Open Memorial Day to Labor Day

The Park offers softball or baseball, batting practice, various games and kiddie rides.

■WESTERLY WINDS GOLF COURSE AND SPORTS PARK
853 Cumberland Street (River Road), Westbrook
207-854-9463
www.golfmaine.com
Open April to October

Westerly Winds has something for everyone with Park 3 Golf, a driving range, miniature golf course, softball and baseball batting cages, a 30'x60' swimming pool, tennis courts and a playground. Kids love climbing and sliding on the twin dinosaurs. The miniature golf course meanders around waterfalls, streams, bridges, ponds and a waterwheel. Finish up at the horseshoe pit, shuffleboard court, basketball court, volleyball court and a soak in the whirlpool. Snacks and sports equipment are available at the Range Shop.

Museums & Educational Adventures

See also; Center for Maine History Museum, and Maine Narrow Gauge Railroad and Museum

■**BRICK STORE MUSEUM**
117 Main Street, Kennebunk
207-985-4802
www.brickstoremuseum.org
Open year-round Tuesday-Friday, 10:00 a.m. to 4:30 p.m;
Saturday, 10:00 a.m. to 1:00 p.m.
Closed all national holidays
Admission is by donation, suggested $3 per person

The museum, dedicated to preserving the cultural heritage of the Kennebunks, consists of four restored nineteenth-century buildings. Discover ship models, paintings and decorative arts, Maine-made crafts as well as books and toys. From June through September the museum sponsors ninety-minute architectural walking tours around the town.

Major exhibitions they have had include Maine Children's Illustrators and Summers at Walker's Point, an historical look at the Bush family's part-time residence here. In fact, former first lady Barbara Bush has been known to drop by and read to children as part of her continuing commitment to literacy. Some one-day events have been a History Workshop to coincide with school's winter vacation, and a Story Camp in July for children ages 8-12.

■CHILDREN'S DISCOVERY MUSEUM
265 Water Street, Augusta
207-622-2209
www.childrensdiscoverymuseum.org
Open year-round. Closed Mondays.
Admission $4 per person; under age 1 free

The Children's Discovery Museum hits the mark with lots of programs and workshops designed for youngsters through grade 5. Children can explore a diner, supermarket, post office, performing stage and river room. They are quickly engrossed with computers, a giant pin-screen and a communications center featuring ham radios, a weather station, satellite tracking and the Internet.

On January 1, 2006 the Museum closed due to lack of staffing combined with financial considerations. But the Board is planning on reopening in the spring of 2006. It would be a shame to lose this wonderful resource in the state's capital city.

■CHILDREN'S MUSEUM OF MAINE
142 Free Street, Portland
207-828-1234
www.kitetails.com
Open year-round.
Labor Day through Memorial Day:
Monday closed to the general public, MEMBERS ONLY
Tuesday-Saturday, 10 a.m. - 5 p.m.
Sunday, noon- 5 p.m.

Memorial Day through Labor Day:
Monday-Saturday, 10 a.m.- 5 p.m.; Sunday, noon-5 p.m.
★First Friday night of each month is FREE from 5-8 p.m.
★Open all week long during school vacations
Admission $6 per person (under age 1 free)
Camera Obscura only: $3.00

It usually takes half an hour to get kids out of the life-size fire truck and move on to the rest of the interactive exhibits in this terrific museum located next to the Portland Museum of Art. Our Town offers the opportunity for young children to do what they do best...use their imaginations in pretend play. They can explore a working ATM, Toddler Park, Grocery Store, Farm, Car Repair Shop, and an animal hospital.

On the Explore Floor, visit L.L. Bear's Discovery Woods and Tree to Timber, a sustainable forestry exhibit. Catch a star lab presentation in the Space Shuttle, check out animal tracks and facts in the Ranger Station, or participate in one of the hands-on art and science projects for kids of all ages that are hosted every day in the Zoom Room. We Are Maine is a new multicultural exhibit exploring the many connections Maine families have to countries around the world.

Been searching for the best view of Portland? The Camera Obscura is one of the city's best kept secrets, and one of only three of its kind in the United States. Exploring Renaissance technology, its connection to the human eye, and its influence on the arts and science, adults and children will find this interesting.

The Explore Store is well stocked with a nice variety of unique educational toys, books and games. There are so many events happening here, we couldn't possibly mention them all. Call for their current events or check the above listed website. You would certainly get your money's worth out of an annual membership here.

From I-295 take exit 6A (Forest Ave. South). Bear right at the lights onto Route 77 South and proceed through the park. Continue up the hill (State Street). At the top of the hill take a left onto Congress Street. Proceed 2/10 mile, cross High Street and immediately bear right onto Free Street.

■GREAT STATE OF MAINE AIR SHOW
Brunswick Naval Air Station, Brunswick
(Take the Cook's Corner exit from Route 1 in Brunswick)
General information: 207-921-2000
www.greatstateofmaineairshow.com
Gates open at 8:00 a.m. Flying starts around 10:00 a.m.
Admission and parking are free

Once a year you get to soar with the eagles while still standing on the ground. This two-day event draws between 160,000 and 200,000 people over a weekend in late summer.

More than forty military and civilian aircraft are on hand, including an F-117 Stealth Fighter. Every few years, the Navy's famous flight demonstration team, The Blue Angels, performs. Thirty tents offer food and souvenirs. Exhibits include simulated aircraft rides and civilian acrobatic acts.

Security regulations require that no backpacks or coolers are allowed inside the gate.

■JOSHUA L. CHAMBERLAIN CIVIL WAR MUSEUM

243 Washington Street, Bath
207-443-1316
www.curtislibrary.com/pejepscot.htm
Open June -October; Tuesday through Saturday
Admission: Adults $5; children $2.50

Joshua Chamberlain (1828-1914) was a Civil War hero at Gettysburg and much of his memorabilia has been preserved here in his partially restored home. The General became famous for his defense of Little Round Top and many of Chamberlain's heroics were recorded in the movie *Gettysburg*. His achievements did not end there. He also served four terms as the governor of Maine. The museum is run by the Pejepscot Historical Society.

■MAINE HISTORICAL SOCIETY MUSEUM

489 Congress Street, Portland
207-774-1822
www.mainehistory.org
Open Monday-Saturday, 10 a.m. to 5 p.m.
Admission: Adults $4; seniors and students $3; children $2; under 5 years of age free

The museum features changing exhibitions and programs spanning more than five centuries of Maine life. Their collections encompass over 2,000 paintings, prints, and other original works of art and approximately 8,000 artifacts.

The diverse collection includes costumes, Native American, military, and domestic artifacts of life in Maine.

A Museum Shop sells books on Maine history as well as unusual gifts with a historic twist. Call or check their website for ongoing educational programs.

■MAINE MARITIME MUSEUM
243 Washington Street, Bath
207-443-1316
www.bathmaine.com
Open year-round, 9:30 a.m. to 5:00 p.m. except Thanksgiving, Christmas and New Year's.
Admission: Adults $9.50; seniors $8.50; children $6.50; under 6 free

Located on the banks of the Kennebec River, the museum offers a treasure trove of boats, art, craftsmanship, history and exploration with regularly changing exhibits and an active waterfront with vessels to watch and explore. Children enjoy the narrated boat cruises, the Lobstering and Maine Coast Exhibit and a special children's play area.

The Museum Book Store and Gift Shop is large, inviting and stocked with a good selection of children's books and games.

■MAINE STATE MUSEUM

State Capital Complex, 83 State House Station, Augusta
207-287-2301
www.state.me.us/museum
Open year-round, daily. Closed all state holidays.
Monday through Friday, 9:00 a.m to 5:00 p.m;
Saturday, 10:00 a.m. to 4:00 p.m;
Sunday, 1:00 p.m. to 4:00 p.m.
Admission: Adults $2; children 6-18; and seniors $1.00;
under age 6 free; family maximum $6.00

Did you know that back in the ice age Maine was covered with a glacier one-mile thick?

For an extensive, well-presented history of all that is Maine, you could not do better than to drive one hour north of Portland to the highly regarded Maine State Museum.

Begin with "12,000 Years in Maine" which focuses on archeology and prehistoric life. Move on through history to the recreated colonial and 19th century homes, shops, and factories surrounding a three-level, operating, water-powered mill. Examine the cargo of the ship St. Mary, one of Maine's last 'Downeasters', and watch a film about the state's timber harvesting, river log drives and sawmill operations.

'Rockhounds' will love the 'Maine Gems' and children are fascinated by the exhibits of native wildlife and their habitats, including trout in a running stream.

From the museum, you can also arrange for a guided or self-guided tour of the State House and Old Fort Western.

The Museum Store has its own coloring book as well as a selection of Maine books, toys, games and other educational items.

■MUSEUM OF AFRICAN CULTURE
122 Spring Street, Portland
(located only one block from the Portland Children's Museum
and the Portland Museum of Art)
207-871-7188
www.tribalartmuseum.com
Open Tuesday through Friday, 10:30 a.m. to 4:00 p.m.;
Saturday, 12:30 p.m. to 4:00 p.m.
Admission: $5.00 donation is requested

Opened in 1998, this is New England's only museum devoted
exclusively to Sub-Saharan African Tribal Art and cultural
traditions.
       Formerly known as The Museum of African Tribal
Art, the small, two-room museum's collection includes masks
and artifacts and ritual objects. The museum offers a number
of public and outreach programs, including performances of
African songs and dance, mask making and painting
workshops.

■MUSICAL WONDER HOUSE
18 High Street, Wiscasset
207-882-7163
www.musicalwonderhouse.com
Open late May to October 31
Guided presentations available daily 10 a.m. to 5 p.m.; after
Labor Day call for schedule
Admission varies by length of the tour

Music boxes, reed organs and other musical instruments make

this historic house appealing.

The shortest presentation costs $10 and lasts for approximately 45 minutes. Many of these instruments are extremely rare and 99% of the collection is in working order.

The Merry Music Box Gift Shop sells music boxes and recordings. AAA lists the Musical Wonder House as one of eight star attractions in Maine.

Wiscasset is about 50 miles north of Portland.

■OLD FORT WESTERN MUSEUM
16 Cony Street, Augusta
207-626-2385
www.oldfortwestern.org
Open Memorial Day-Labor Day, 10 a.m. to 4 p.m. daily;
Labor Day to Columbus Day, 1 p.m. to 4 p.m. weekends only;
November, December, January: first Sunday of the month;
March - Maple Syrup Day (fourth Sunday of the month)
Admission: Adults $5; seniors 55 and over $4;
children ages 6-16 $3; under age 6 and Augusta residents free

Experience every day life at Fort Western and the Howard Store as it was from 1754 to 1810. Costumed characters engage in typical 18th century chores, make crafts and answer questions. Located on the east bank of the Kennebec River, this is the oldest surviving fort in New England.

Children are fascinated by the stockade. The museum hosts several interesting and educational events. It is well worth your while to go on-line or call and request a schedule.

Old Fort Western Museum
Kennebec River

■OLD LINCOLN COUNTY JAIL & MUSEUM
Route 218, Federal Street, Wiscasset
207-882-6817
www.lincolncountyhistory.org/lchaparts/oldjail.htm
Open June and September, Saturdays, 10 a.m. to 4 p.m.
July and August, Tues-Sat., 10 a.m to 4 p.m
October through May, by appointment only
Admission: Adults $4; children $2

A stark view of prison life in the 19th century. Children love to clamber around and explore the prisoners' cells with the original graffiti still on the walls.

The Jailor's House contains an early 19th century kitchen and an exhibit of antique tools.

■PEARY-MACMILLAN ARCTIC MUSEUM & ARCTIC STUDIES CENTER
Bowdoin College, Brunswick
207-725-3416
www.academic.bowdoin.edu/arcticmuseum
Open Tuesday through Saturday, 10:00 a.m. to 5:00 p.m.
Sunday, 2:00 p.m. to 5:00 p.m. Closed Mondays and National Holidays

The museum is located on the main floor of Hubbard Hall on the beautiful Bowdoin College campus. Its mission is to promote understanding of and appreciation for the cultures and natural environments found in Arctic regions.

Items from Bowdoin graduates Robert E. Peary and Donald B. MacMillan's excursions, such as fur clothing, snowshoes and pick axes are on display. You can see the sled that took Peary to the North Pole in 1909.

Collections include exploration equipment, natural history specimens, artifacts, art, still photographs, motion picture films, recordings and publications. Kids gravitate to the stuffed polar bears, Inuit folk art and narwhal tusks.

The Arctic Museum Gift Shop carries an excellent selection of children's books, Arctic animal puppets, puzzles and masks.

Can't get there in person? Visit their website and take the online virtual tour.

■PINE TREE STATE ARBORETUM
153 Hospital Street, Augusta
207-621-0031
www.pinetreestatearboretum.org
Open year-round, dawn to dusk, seven days a week
Admission free

This beautiful 224-acre arboretum lists education as a large part of its mission. The Johnson Outdoor Education Center was opened in 1997 and is made up of eleven outdoor classrooms that present interesting exhibits relating to the forest's ecosystem and products and also serve as a source of recreation. A self-guided tour is free or an activity filled Learning Guide for all ages can be purchased at their Visitor Center.

They offer programs for young people on Wildlife Habitat, Ecosystems, Pond Life, Wetland Studies, Tree Identification and Forest Management to name just a few.

Some winter programs include Snowshoe Adventure, Animals Tracks and Signs, and Plants in Winter.

This is a tremendously interesting spot and you and your children are bound to come away having learned a great deal.

Picnicking is permitted and their marked 5-mile trail system is open year-round for hiking, jogging, bird watching, non-motorized biking, horseback riding, and cross-country skiing.

Guided tours and activities are also available for groups upon request.

■PORTLAND HARBOR MUSEUM
Southern Maine Community College Campus
Fort Road, South Portland
207-799-6337
www.portlandharbormuseum.org
Open April and May, Friday-Sunday, 10 a.m.- 4:30 p.m.
June-October, daily, 10 a.m.- 4:30 p.m.
October- Thanksgiving, Friday-Sunday, 10 a.m.- 4:00 p.m
Admission: Adults $4, students and children free

Portland Harbor Museum lies within the granite walls of 19th century Fort Preble and boasts a dramatic oceanfront setting. The museum features changing exhibits on local maritime history and a restoration of the *Snow Squall*, an 1850s Portland clipper ship that was wrecked in the Falkland Islands.

What really makes this spot special for the younger set is that you can walk from the museum out to the 900-foot breakwater that juts into Casco Bay to the Spring Point Ledge Lighthouse. Children love to play around the historic fort where many of the coast artillery gun emplacements from both World Wars are still visible.

A walking tour guide of the area is available at the museum. The well-marked Spring Point Shoreline Walkway is at the museum's doorstep and offers an annotated walk by Casco Bay, Portland Head Light and Portland Breakwater's "Bug" Light. Bring swimsuits in the summer as the sandy shore of Willard Beach is also easily accessible from the walkway.

A gift shop is open during museum hours and has a nice selection of items for children.

■PORTLAND MUSEUM OF ART
7 Congress Street, Portland
207-775-6148
www.portlandmuseum.org
Open year-round.
Tues., Wed., Thurs., Sat., Sun.,: 10 a.m. - 5 p.m.
Fri.: 10 a.m.- 9 p.m.
Open Mondays: 10 a.m.-5 p.m.
Closed New Years Day, Thanksgiving and Christmas
Admission: Members free
Adults $8; seniors and students with I.D. $6;
children 6-17, $2; children under 6 free
Free admission Friday evenings, 5 p.m.- 9 p.m.

Celebrate world-class art at the Portland Museum's postmodern building, designed in 1983 by Henry Cobb of

The I.M.Pei architectural firm. An unparalleled look at three centuries of works by Winslow Homer, John Singer Sargent, Rockwell Kent, Mardsen Hartley, and Andrew Wyeth. European movements are represented by works of Auguste Renoir, Edgar Degas, Claude Monet, Pablo Picasso, Eduard Munch, and Rene Magritte.

Hands-on studio classes are offered for preschool kids where children (with a parent/guardian) take a brief tour of the museum before sitting down at the PMA's Community Studio with some clay or a paint brush.

There is a café and a museum shop that are both open to the public with no admission. Check for frequently scheduled lectures, workshops and Family Days.

■PORTLAND PUBLIC MARKET
25 Preble Street, Portland
207-228-2000
www.portlandmarket.com
Open daily, year-round. Monday-Saturday, 7 a.m.-7 p.m.
Sunday, 10 a.m.- 5 p.m.
Closed most state holidays.

Make your way to this wonderful renovated brick and glass two-story building to wander through aisles of all the best Maine foods fresh from the producers.

You can buy almost anything here from fantastic homemade breads, fresh fruits, all manner of deserts and meats and condiments and flowers. This is how the Europeans love to shop - the freshest ingredients.

The Market has dozens of interesting classes suitable

for young people in the fall, winter and spring that are taught in their state-of-the-art demonstration kitchen on the mezzanine level. Call (207) 228-2001 or check their website to register for classes.

Park outdoors at the Public Market Garage. Tip: Park on level 3 and walk across the enclosed skybridge to the market. Take your parking ticket to be stamped by the vendors.

■SEASHORE TROLLEY MUSEUM
195 Log Cabin Road, Kennebunkport
207-967-2712 or 207-967-2800
www.trolleymuseum.org
Open early May and late October, Saturday and Sunday only
Memorial Day through Columbus Day, daily 10 a.m. to 5 p.m.
Last tour at 4:15 p.m.
Admission: Adults $8; seniors $6; children 6-16 $5.50;
under 5 free

Ride along the former Atlantic Shoreline trolley line for nearly four miles with a stop along the way at the museum's restoration shop, where you will see old trolleys made new. The museum has a collection of 200 streetcars from major cities and world capitals as diverse as San Francisco and Budapest.

Founded in 1939, it offers a glimpse at a disappearing way of life and is the world's oldest and largest museum of mass transit vehicles. At 7:00 p.m. every Wednesday and Thursday evening in July and August, there is an Ice Cream and Sunset Trolley Ride Special for $4.00 per person (ice cream included).

Special events include the Kennebunkport Holiday Prelude Celebration during the first two weekends in December and a fall Pumpkin Patch Trolley Weekend. A museum store, snacks and restrooms are available.

■SOUTHWORTH PLANETARIUM
96 Falmouth Street, Science Building
University of Southern Maine, Portland
207-780-4249 Skywatch Hotline: 207-780-4719
www.usm.maine.edu/planet
Open year-round. Astronomy shows, Friday and Saturday at 7 p.m. and 8:30 p.m; Saturday matinees, 3:00 p.m.
October through March they offer Sunday matinees, 3:00 p.m.
Call ahead for information and newly offered shows.

"Greetings, stargazers....."call the Skywatch Hotline for updates on the astronomical events occurring that week with a new episode recorded each Sunday.

This intimate 63-seat theater offers a universe of wonders for all ages. They have numerous well thought out shows for children including astronomy shows such as *ABC's of the Sky,* and *The Little Star.* Holiday Special Shows are presented around Halloween and Christmas. The elaborate multimedia astronomy show is followed by the current night's sky being projected on the 30-foot dome. Leave time to wander through the exhibit area where interactive computers allow you to explore space. Watch shuttle launches on their video monitors and visit their expansive gift shop.

■STATE HOUSE
Capital Complex, Augusta
207-287-2301
Tours are available year-round

Designed in 1829 by noted architect Charles Bulfinch, the State House dome rises 185 feet. Offering a good look into the workings of our state government, the building houses both the executive and legislative branches.

Augusta is only 57 miles north of Portland and you might combine this experience with a trip to the Children's Discovery Museum, Old Fort Western, or the Pine Tree State Arboretum.

■TOM'S OF MAINE
27 Community Drive, Kennebunk
207-985-2944 or 800-775-2388
www.tomsofmaine.com
Factory tours given in the summer only.
Monday through Thursday: 9:30, 10:30, 1:00 and 2:00;
Friday, 9:30 and 10:30
Reservations are required

Some of the best segments on Sesame Street are when they show how things (i.e. crayons, paper) are actually made from start to finish. Well, how about toothpaste?

Tom's of Maine is well-known for their toothpastes, deodorants, soaps and shampoos, all made with only pure, natural ingredients. Factory tours take about 45 minutes. Visitors view the Quality Control Lab and Make areas before ending up in the manufacturing area. The company does not recommend tours for children under the age of 5.

Visit the website for an online factory tour.

■WELLS ANTIQUE AUTO MUSEUM
Route 1, 1181 Post Road, Wells
207-646-9064
Open daily, Memorial Day to Columbus Day, 10 a.m.- 5 p.m
Admission: Adults $5; children $2; under 6 free

Take a little spin in a restored Model T and look over the 80 or so vintage cars, including a Stanley Steamer, a Stutz Bearcat and a 1908 Baker Electric car once owned by J.D. Rockefeller.

They also have motorcycles, old auto signs, vintage bicycles and a great collection of nickelodeon machines that actually work (for a dime or a quarter).

Theater & Dance

■ARUNDEL BARN PLAYHOUSE
53 Old Post Road, Arundel
207-985-5552
www.arundelbarnplayhouse.com
Open mid-June to end of August

The Playhouse offers five professional, musical theatre productions, each running two or three weeks. Located in an 1800s farm barn that was recycled as a live theater in 1998 adds charm and atmosphere to each event. Some past productions include *Oliver* and *Hello Dolly!*

■BATES DANCE FESTIVAL
Bates College, Schaeffer Theater, Lewiston
207-786-6161
www.bates.edu

Bates College sponsors this annual month-long celebration every summer, featuring dance performances, workshops, lectures and concerts.
    Started in 1982, the festival has achieved national recognition offering postmodern, jazz, improvisational and flamenco performances.

This annual festival consists of interwoven programs: two professional training programs that include the Young Dancers' Workshop (YDW), a rigorous two-week program serving pre-professional dancers ages 13-17; and community outreach activities including the Youth Arts Program serving local youth ages 6-17 with dance and music training.

■CASCO BAY MOVERS DANCE STUDIO
517 Forest Avenue, Portland
207-871-1013
www.cascobaymovers.com
Year-round programs for kids and adults

This group puts on some of the most fun, toe-tapping exhibitions in town. We highly recommend you call and see if they are performing at a time convenient for your family. They offer children's programs that include jazz, street funk, tap, ballet, choreography and even break dancing. They are available for birthday parties as well.

■CENTER FOR CULTURAL EXCHANGE
One Longfellow Square, Portland
Main Office: 207-767-0591   Box Office: 207-761-1545
www.centerforculturalexchange.com

The Exchange is a not-for-profit institution dedicated to advancing cultural understanding through arts and education programs. They host over 200 events each year. Kinder-Culture is for kids 3-8 years old and includes hands-on activities in art, puppetry, stories and dance. They celebrate diversity with year-round performances, workshops, dances, ethnic meals, and festivals.

■CENTER FOR THE ARTS AT THE CHOCOLATE CHURCH
798 Washington Street, Bath
207-442-8455
www.chocolatechurcharts.org

This lovely converted (chocolate-colored) church offers year-round entertainment. The Center puts on a variety of shows that range from an *a capella* group to family bluegrass. They produce a holiday concert at Christmas and in 1999 began a Youth Theatre group with the *Wizard of Oz* as their first production. A variety of special programs for children are offered in this 100-seat theater.

■CHILDREN'S THEATER OF MAINE
317 Marginal Way, Portland
Ticket info: 207-828-0617
General info: 207-878-2774
Admission: Adults $8; children $6

One of the oldest children's theaters in the country, CTM produces classic fairy tales, contemporary children's stories and the winning script from its Annual Young Playwright's Contest during the school year.

This much-loved institution features live music as

well as wonderful, professional quality costumes, sets and lighting designs. They host an annual Shakespeare Festival each spring, where high schools from around the state perform.

CTM sponsors the Annual Playwright's Contest, where children age 18 or younger can submit their plays. The winning plays are produced every spring. Bravo CMT for providing high quality fare *and* opportunity for our young people!

■CITY THEATER
205 Main Street, Biddeford
207-282-0849
www.citytheater.org

Part of the area's vibrant community theater scene, City Theater offers a series of live performances in their 660-seat historic building that was once the Biddeford Opera House.

Some of their past productions include *Forever Plaid, Lazer Vaudeville, Rocky Horror Show* and *Carousel.*

■DEERTREES THEATRE & CULTURAL CENTER
Deertrees Road, Harrison
207-583-4533 or 207-583-6747
www.deertreestheatre.org
Open June to Labor Day. Evening shows begin at 8 p.m except Sundays at 7 p.m.
Children's Wednesday productions at 10 a.m. and 1 p.m.

This historic theater, on the National Register of Historic Places, is home to the acclaimed Sebago-Long Lakes Region Music Festival. They also offer dance performances, concerts, theatrical productions and children's shows.

The Figures of Speech Theatre troupe of puppetry has performed here as has The Portland Symphony.

Call for listings that feature such diverse treats as *a capella,* classical, Negro spirituals, and jazz musicians.

This 500-seat opera house will host over 30 events in the summer. Picnicking is encouraged on the Deertrees grounds before the performance. Or buy a snack at the Salt Lick Café, so named because when the theater was built, the deer would come and feed at a salt lick on the property.

■FIGURES OF SPEECH THEATRE
77 Durham Road, Freeport
207-865-6355
www.figures.org

This exuberantly unique puppetry-based, touring theater company is a result of a husband and wife who are a sculptor and a costume designer, respectively. Actors perform in gorgeous, elaborate costumes with large, hand-carved puppets to original, live music. The plays are staged in various theaters. St. Lawrence Arts Center in Portland hosted the production of *Far East - Tales from China and Japan.* Other productions that they perform include *The Beanstalk Variations,* and *The Nightingale.*

Call for a list of locations for upcoming shows.

■HACMATACK PLAYHOUSE
538 School Street (Route 9), Berwick
207-698-1807
www.hackmatack.org
Open June through August, Wed.-Sat. at 8:00 p.m.
Thursday Matinee 2:00 p.m.
Admission: Adult $20; seniors $17; students (under 20) $10.
Reservations recommended..

Hackmatack has produced *Joseph and the Amazing Technicolor Dreamcoat, Oliver!* and *The Secret Garden.* This former barn house has been remodeled with a stage and real theater seats.

Don't miss home-grown sweet strawberries and shortcake served during intermission.

During July and August there is a children's theater series with such hits as *Charlie and the Chocolate Factory* and *A Star Spangled Journey.*

■HAMILTON HOUSE
40 Vaughan's Lane, South Berwick
207-384-2454
www.spnea.org/visit/homes/hamilton.htm
Open June 1 through October 15; Wednesday through Sunday; grounds open dawn to dusk
Admission: $8

Hamilton House, overlooking the Salmon Falls River, is operated by The Society for the Preservation of New England Antiquities.

Come on a Sunday in July with a picnic and enjoy one of their summer concerts. Ask for a schedule of events for children.

■KINDERKONZERTS
Merrill Auditorium, Portland
207-773-6128
www.portlandsymphony.com/education.lasso
Admission $3

The Portland Symphony Orchestra has a long history of bringing the power of live orchestral music to children through its Kinderkonzerts, Youth Concerts, and other educational programs.

Kinderkonzerts explore the different families of orchestral instruments with children ages four to seven while introducing them to live symphonic music through interactive programs.

Youth Concerts, also held at the magnificently restored Merrill Auditorium, help to introduce 8 to 13 year-old children to the Portland Symphony.

■LYRIC MUSIC THEATER
176 Sawyer Street, South Portland
207-856-1663   Box Office: 207-774-2435
www.lyricmusictheater.com
Open September through May
Friday & Saturday 8:00 p.m.; Sunday Matinee 2:30 p.m
Admission Friday & Saturday $19; Sunday Matinee $17

This community theater produces four musicals a year that are often suitable for children. In the past they have offered up *The Sound of Music, Hello, Dolly!, West Side Story* and *The Wizard of Oz.*

■MAINE STATE BALLET
91 Forest Street, Westbrook
207-856-1663 or 207-842-0800
www.mainestateballet.org

This semi-professional company performs classic, full-length ballets at least twice a year at Portland's Merrill Auditorium. They produce *The Nutcracker* during the holiday season and in the spring put on ballets such as *Alice in Wonderland, Hansel and Gretel* and *Sleeping Beauty.*

■MAINE STATE MUSIC THEATRE
22 Elm Street, Brunswick
207-725-8769
www.msmt.org
Performances from early June through August
Admission varies from $17 to $35, depending on the day and the seat location. No children under the age of four are allowed at any plays except the Children's Theater productions.

The MSMT, one of the state's most renowned summer theater groups, inaugurated a newly renovated, air-conditioned facility in 2003. Some of the 2006 productions included *South*

Pacific, Beauty and the Beast and *Aida.* Consider combining a show with a visit to the Peary-MacMillan Arctic Museum, located on the Bowdoin College campus.

They stage two productions a year that are specifically for children.

■OGUNQUIT PLAYHOUSE

Route 1, Ogunquit
Box Office: 207-646-5511   Other Info: 207-646-2403
www.ogunquitplayhouse.org
Open late June to Labor Day
Performances at 8:00 p.m.
Kids' Korner shows Saturday at noon

The Ogunquit Playhouse is one of the country's oldest summer theaters, offering plays and light musicals that draw national talent and a multi-generational audience.

Saturday Kids' Korner has shows at noon during the summer. Shows they have put on include *James and the Giant Peach, Madeline, Stuart Little* and *Jack and the Beanstalk.* Adding to the fun are picnics before each show held in The Gazebo Garden beginning at 10:30 a.m. Admission is free with that day's Kids' Korner Theater ticket and children enjoy face painting, games and a craft.

■PORTLAND BALLET COMPANY

517 Forest Avenue, Portland
207-772-9671
www.portlandballet.org

The Portland Ballet Company produces both classical and contemporary pieces, often at The Merrill Auditorium, but occasionally elsewhere such as Portland High School. At Christmas they stage *A Victorian Nutcracker,* commemorating the Victoria Mansion in Portland. Other productions have included *Cinderella,* and *Peter and the Wolf.*

■PORTLAND CONCERT ASSOCIATION GREAT PERFORMANCES
Merrill Auditorium, 477 Congress Street, Portland
Porttix (the box office for Merrill Auditorium and home to PCA Great Performances and the Portland Symphony Orchestra) 207-842-0800 or www.porttix.com
Open year-round
Admission prices vary with the performance and seating

Merrill Auditorium, the old City Hall, has been completely refurbished into a truly dazzling, world-class concert hall with great acoustics, wonderful sight-lines and comfortable seats. A diverse and exciting calendar brings live performances of some of the world's foremost artists: Yo-Yo Ma, The Dance Theater of Harlem and the Russian National Ballet. Some of the PCA Great Performances have been Roald Dahl's *Willy Wonka, Swan Lake,* and *Thumbilina.*

The schedule is very fluid, so call or check online for current and upcoming performances.

■PORTLAND OPERA REPERTORY THEATRE
437 Congress Street, Portland
Tickets: 207-842-0800   General Info: 207-879-7678
www.portopera.org

Port Opera stages productions such as *La Boheme, Carmen* and *Madame Butterfly* at the beautifully restored Merrill Auditorium. They produce an Opera Festival every summer.

■PORTLAND PLAYERS
Thaxter Theater, 420 Cottage Road, South Portland
207-799-7338
www.portlandplayers.org
Productions September through June

Community Theater offering fine productions of shows such as *Oliver!, Godspell,* and *Gypsy.*

■PORTLAND STAGE COMPANY
25A Forest Avenue, Portland
Box Office: 207-774-0465   General Info: 207-774-1043
www.portlandstage.com
Admission Adults $25-$35; seniors/students $20-$30

PSC stages about six professionally produced shows from October through May, with special shows during the summer season. The production of *A Christmas Carol* throughout the month of December has become a popular local tradition.

■SACO DRIVE-IN THEATER
969 Portland Road (Route 1), Saco
207-284-1016
Double features from May to September
Gates open at 7:30 p.m. and the show starts at dusk

I almost listed this under the history section but then thought better of it. Yes, it's true, the area still offers one of the few remaining drive-in theaters in the state.

Put the kids in their pajamas and take them to enjoy a double feature, sprawled out under the stars with a huge screen looming down. Break down when they show those old intermission advertisements and let them enjoy some popcorn, soda and hot dogs dripping with yellow mustard.

Unlike the old days when you had to remember to put the speaker back before heading home, you now get the sound from a special station on your radio.

If you don't like what's playing there, Westbrook has the Pride's Corner Drive-In (207-797-3154) on Route 302.

■STAGE AT SPRING POINT
Fort Preble, South Portland
207-828-0128
www.thestagemaine.org
Admission free (donations accepted)

Free outdoor theater, sparkling productions, imaginative costuming and a delightful musical score acted by a professional theater company intent on bringing classics to the local community.

The company performs a selection once-a-year outdoors at Fort Preble's Battery Rivardi on the Southern Maine Community College campus in South Portland. There are 120 seats.

Past productions have included *The Miser* by Moliere and Shakespeare's *MacBeth.*

■SUMMER IN THE PARKS' CONCERTS
Information: 207-756-8275
Cancellation Line: 207-756-8130
All concerts are free.
If it rains, concerts are cancelled.

Portland Parks and Recreation Department, along with area businesses, sponsors a series of free arts and music performances in various Portland Parks.

★ Tuesday Night Concerts at Deering Oaks Park Bandstand: July through August around 7:00 p.m.

★ Sunset Folk Series, Wednesdays at the Western Prom Park: July through mid-August, starting between 7:30 and 8:00 p.m

★ Thursday Kids' Concerts Series at Deering Oaks Park Bandstand: July and August at 12:30 p.m.

★ Nostalgia Night at Fort Allen Park Gazebo on the Eastern Prom: three Thursday nights in July. Call for exact dates and times.

★ Fourth of July Festival: 7 p.m. to 10 p.m at the Eastern Prom. Food vendors and fireworks display.

■THE THEATER AT MONMOUTH
Main Street, Route 132, Monmouth
Open May through the fall
Box Office: 207-933-9999 (opens June 1st)
www.theateratmonmouth.org

This acclaimed theater presents the world's great plays in rotating repertory. Known as The Shakespearean Theater of Maine, productions are staged in the Victorian Opera House Cumston Hall. While they are famous for extraordinary productions of *A Midsummer Night's Dream, Hamlet,* and *Shadowland* they also offer young children's shows such as *Aladdin, Rumplestiltskin,* and *Alice in Woderland.*
    Monmouth is about one hour northwest of Portland.

■THE THEATER PROJECT
14 School Street, Brunswick
207-729-8584
www.theaterproject.com
Open year-round
All tickets are 'pay-what-you-want' (donations accepted)

Located in the heart of downtown Brunswick in a beautifully preserved building, The Theater Project offers new and classic plays, year-round classes for adults, teenagers and school-age actors and community festivals.
    During the holiday season they produce old favorites as well as new productions. The traditional holiday show, *Wales, Tunes & Tales* features holiday music and *A Child's Christmas in Wales.*

A Nod to History

See also Burnt Island Lighthouse

■BOOTHBAY RAILWAY VILLAGE
Route 27, Boothbay Harbor
207-633-4727
www.railwayvillage.org
Open Memorial Day through Columbus Day,
9:30 a.m. to 5:00 p.m.; last train runs at 4:00 p.m.
Admission: Adults $8; children 3 -16 $4

This historic recreated early New England village has 27 exhibit buildings located on 30 acres.

Various types of transportation are highlighted, but also located on the property are a one-room school house, bank, barbershop, millinery and village Toy Shop.

Ride a narrow gauge steam train for 1 ½ miles to the village's exceptional antique auto display. Over 60 restored vehicles demonstrate the evolution of wheeled transportation from horse and buggy to steam trains and Model T Fords.

Call or visit the website of this non-profit organization for a schedule of events. Look for the Ghost Train at Halloween.

The third Sunday in August is Children's Day when all children under 12 are admitted free when accompanied by an adult.

■COLONIAL PEMAQUID RESTORATION
Off Route 130, New Harbor
207-677-2423
www.maine.gov/doc/parks/programs/history/pemaquid/greeting.
htm
Open Memorial Day to Labor Day, 9:00 a.m. to 5:00 p.m
Admission: $2.00 for ages 12-64; all others free

Founded in 1692, Fort Pemaquid is the site of a very early English outpost and fishing station. Today, Colonial Pemaquid is a State Historic Site owned and managed by the Bureau of Parks and Lands.

Archaeologists have unearthed the remains of the 17th century site and inside the museum you can explore the 1620s settlement with dioramas and artifacts uncovered from the area.

A museum shop is located in the Fort House and an adjacent seafood restaurant and picnic area have a lovely view of the quiet harbor.

In the past, they have hosted the Maine Heritage Days in mid-September to commemorate the events that occurred in 1747 during the colonial wars between France and England with living history portrayals and demonstrations.

If you would like to combine this visit with a swim, Pemaquid Beach Park in Bristol is a lovely swimming beach nearby with bathhouses, restrooms and a concession stand.

■GHOSTLY TOURS
Rte. 1A, 250 York Street, York
207-363-0000
www.ghostlytours.com
Open June through October 30th
Tickets go on sale one hour before the tour begins
Reservations are strongly recommended
Admission: $10 per person

This is a great way to combine a little spooky fun with a little history. Ghostly Tours will lead you and your family on a candlelight tour through Old York Village. Your hooded tour guide will thrill youngsters with authentic ghost stories, witch tales and folklore of the 18th and 19th centuries.

The tour is not just fictional tales, the proprietors say that every hair-raising story is documented in old newspapers and journals.

■HARRIET BEECHER STOW HOUSE
63 Federal Street, Brunswick

Harriet Beecher Stowe wrote *Uncle Tom's Cabin*, the book some people say started the Civil War, while living here at her Federal Street home. The mother of six young children resided in Brunswick from 1850 to 1852 while her husband taught at Bowdoin College nearby.

Her home has been turned into an inn and restaurant and is one of 24 stops on *A Woman's History Walking Trail,* a brochure available from the Pejepscot Historical Society (207-729-6606). It's never too early to inspire our daughters.

■MAINE NARROW GAUGE RAILROAD CO. AND MUSEUM

58 Fore Street, Portland
207-828-0814
www.mngrr.org
Open year-round except January to mid-February. Museum open daily, 10:00 a.m. to 4:00 p.m. Train rides are on the hour beginning at 11:00 a.m.
Admission: Adults $8; seniors $7; children under 3 free

Dedicated to preserving Maine narrow gauge railroad equipment, this collection was moved to Maine in 1993 from the Edaville RR in Massachusetts. Trains include closed-in coaches and open cars built for excursion service.

The tracks start at the Fore Street Marina and ring Portland's Eastern Promenade as they travel 1 ½ miles along the shore of Casco Bay.

In October they hold the Ghost Train with rides running all afternoon and evening and costume contests.

Special events also include a Santa Fest and *The Polar Express* in December.

■NARRAMISSIC FARM

Ingalls Road, South Bridgton
207-647-3699 or 207-647-2765
Open mid-June and August; Wednesday through Monday (closed Tuesdays)
Admission: $5 per person; $12 maximum per family

This historic 1797 farm, now run by the Bridgton Historical

Society, has been lovingly restored to the way it appeared on the eve of the Civil War.

The farm includes a working barn and a blacksmith shop. There are many demonstrations here and they also host several special events such as a Civil War Reenactment, a Harvest Festival and Christmas Open House. The gift shop sells old-fashioned toys and books.

Bridgton is approximately 34 miles west of Portland on Route 302.

■OLD YORK
Lindsay Road and Route 1A, York
207-367-4974
www.oldyork.org
Open early June to Columbus Day; Monday through Saturday, 10:00 a.m. to 5 p.m.; closed Sundays
Admission: Adults $5 one building, $10 all buildings; seniors $4 one building, $8 all buildings; children under 16 $3 one building, $5 all buildings; under age 4 free

Run by the Old York Historical Society, Old York's focus is on life in Maine from the mid-1600s on. It consists of 7 historic buildings and offers living history demonstrations, guided tours, and self-guided walks. You will meet the jailer's family, the tavern keeper and the school master.

Kids like having their pictures taken on the pillory in front of the Old Gaol (jail). Old York was the King's Prison for the Province of Maine in the early 1700s.

They have their own Education Department that works hard developing programs like Living History, Young

Travelers and Explorer's Camp. Many hands-on exhibits and a wide variety of children's workshops and activities take place all summer.

■PORTLAND OBSERVATORY
138 Congress Street, Portland
207-774-5561
www.portlandlandmarks.org
Open Memorial Day through Columbus Day (closed July 4)
Guided tours offered daily 10 a.m. - 5 p.m.
Admission: Adults $5; under 16 $3; under 6 free

On a clear day you can see forever after climbing up the stairway to the deck of this 82-foot octagonal tower that once notified Portlanders of incoming ships. Built in 1807 when Portland's harbor was aflutter with the white sails of trading ships, the observatory has been lovingly restored and is now staffed by Greater Portland Landmarks.

There are exhibits, guided tours, gifts and one-of-a-kind views of the city and Casco Bay.

■SABBATHDAY LAKE SHAKER VILLAGE AND COMMUNITY
707 Shaker Road (Rte. 26), New Gloucester
207-926-4597
www.shaker.lib.me.us
Open Memorial Day through Columbus Day,
10 a.m. to 4:30 p.m. daily, closed Sundays
Admission: Adults $6.50; under 12 $2.00

Twenty-five miles north of Portland you can step into the living history of the Shakers. Exhibits of Shaker life from the 1700s to the present day include a schoolhouse, library, sisters' shop, herb house, spin house and gardens.

Browse through the museum, museum shop and the Shaker store. This is the last remaining active Shaker village in the world and the great simplicity that informs their lives is truly remarkable. Shakers have always welcomed the outside world and, in these sometimes overstimulated times our children live in, it's nice to spend an afternoon with the people whose most well-known song is *Simple Gifts.* Take the Maine Turnpike to exit 63 (Gray) and proceed to Route 26 north.

Inquire about special workshops, fairs and concerts.

■TATE HOUSE
1270 Westbrook Street, Portland
207-774-6177
www.tatehouse.org
Open June 15 to September 30, Tuesday through Sunday and weekends through October. Closed Mondays.
Tuesday through Saturday, 10 a.m. to 4 p.m.
Sundays, 1- 4 p.m.
Admission: Adults $7; seniors (65+) $5; children under 12 $2; children under 6 free

Built by Captain George Tate in 1755, this is the only pre-Revolutionary home in Greater Portland open to the public. Wander through the beautiful raised-bed herb gardens in summer.

Also, inquire about the occasional craft demonstrations and activities for children in the summer months. If you think you saw a ghost, perhaps it was the late Mrs. Tate who was murdered by one of her sons!

They always have available 18th century children's games to play and a historical scavenger hunt.

■WADSWORTH-LONGFELLOW HOUSE
489 Congress Street, Portland
207-774-1822
www.mainehistory.org
Open May through December, daily
Admission: Adults $7; seniors and students $6; children $3

The famous poet's childhood home, built in 1786, is part of and next door to The Center for Maine History. The brick house is still furnished in authentic early American style. Take time to enjoy the lovely little garden next to the Maine Historical Societies Library and to browse in their gift shop.

There is no better time to visit than during December when it's dressed up as if magically returned to a nineteenth century Christmas.

Longfellow was America's most popular poet by the mid-19th century, and he produced poems that many of us still know by heart; *Paul Revere's Ride, The Courtship of Miles Standish, Evangeline, The Song of Hiawatha, The Village Blacksmith* and *The Children's Hour.*

The Children's Hour
(Excerpted from Henry Wadsworth Longfellow)

Between the dark and the daylight
When the night is beginning to lower,
Comes a pause in the day's occupations,
That is known as the Children's Hour.

I hear in the chamber above me
The patter of little feet,
The sound of a door that is opened,
And voices soft and sweet.

I have you fast in my fortress
And will not let you depart,
But put you down into the dungeon
In the round-tower of my heart.

And there will I keep you forever,
Yes forever and a day,
Till the walls shall crumble to ruin
And moulder in dust away!

■WASHBURN-NORLANDS LIVING HISTORY CENTER
Route108, 290 Norlands Road, Livermore
207-897-4366
www.norlands.org
Open July and August, Monday through Saturday, 10 a.m. to 4 p.m.; Sunday, 1:00 p.m to 6:00 p.m.

Call for off-season schedule.
Admission varies by program.

Enter this restored 19th century property and you are transported to another age. The 445-acre working farm and museum include a library, church, barn and a schoolhouse.

Norlands is high on the list of "educational vacations" where you can make reservations to live-in for one or two days. Live-in visitors are given a 19th century character whose identity they assume (name and all) and whose life and chores they carry out during their stay. Once transported back to the era 1870 to 1890, your family will go about life as it was.

Take in Christmas at Norlands and go on a jingle bell ride, sing carols in the 1800s church and visit the museum shop for old-fashioned stocking stuffers.

Norlands is about 90 minutes north of Portland.

■WILLOWBROOK AT NEWFIELD
RESTORATION VILLAGE
68 Elm Street, Route 11, Newfield
207-793-2784
www.willowbrookmuseum.org
Open daily, May 15 to September 30, 10 a.m. to 5 p.m.
Admission: Adults $8.50; seniors 65+ $7.50; children 6 to 18 $4.00; under 6 free

Willowbrook at Newfield is the largest 19th century museum village in America and is listed on the National Register of Historic Places. The country Victorian era comes to life here as children can leisurely view a restored carousel, school house, the second oldest Concord coach in existence and an 1832 country store.

An extensively furnished Children's Room offers a look into what kids used to play with before computers and ipods. A highlight of the village is The Toy Shop and the Silas P. Hardy Bicycle Shop.

There are 37 buildings and exhibits to visit plus an old-fashioned ice cream shop and the Sandwich Shoppe for a sweet treat or a well-rounded meal. A picnic area is available as well as a Christmas Etcetera gift shop.

Kids love picking out penny candy from the Amos Straw Country Store.

Willowbrook is a 35-mile drive due west of Portland. Driving time is about one hour.

Room for Notes

So many books....so little time.

Booking It

Maine's literary history is extensive with many authors living in and/or writing about our Pine Tree State. Kate Douglas Wiggin (1856-1923) grew up in Hollis and her beloved children's book, *Rebecca of Sunnybrook Farm*, was set nearby. Henry Wadsworth Longfellow (1807-1882) wrote many poems based on Maine themes. Some of his best-known include, *Evangeline, The Lighthouse, The Ropewalk, The Building of the Ship, The Rainy Day, Keramos, The Baron of St. Castine,* and *The Courtship of Miles Standish*. In *My Lost Youth,* he evokes Portland as it was over 100 years ago:

> *I remember the black wharves and the slips.*
> *And the sea-tides tossing free;*
> *And Spanish sailors with bearded lips,*
> *And the beauty and mystery of the ships,*
> *And the magic of the sea.*

Of the many charming picture books for children that are set in Maine, those of the late Robert McClosky are certainly some of the most enduring. Any Maine library or book store should have the following McClosky classics: *One Morning in Maine, Time of Wonder, Blueberries for Sal, Homer Price,* and *Burt Dow: Deep-Water Man.*

Barbara Cooney (1917-2000), twice a winner of the prestigious Caldecott Medal, lived in Damariscotta. Her acclaimed books *Island Boy* and *Miss Rumphius* are surely inspired by her home state.

For a listing of over 185 Maine children's books including author and illustrator biographies, check out Lynn Plourde and Paul Knowles guide, *A Celebration of Maine Children's Books* (University of Maine Press).

Here are some other suggestions that our family and friends have enjoyed:

Birdie's Lighthouse, by Deborah Hopkinson, Atheneum Books for Young Readers, Simon & Schuster.

Good Golly Miss Molly and the 4th of July Parade: Her Story, by Eloise Enser, Windswept House Publishers.

The Great State of Maine Activity Book, by Jane Petrlik Smolik, MidRun Press

Do Whales Ever...What You Really Want to Know About Whales, Porpoises and Dolphins, by Nathalie Ward, Down East Books.

Project Puffin: How We Brought Puffins Back to Egg Rock, by Stephen W. Kress, as told to Pete Salmansohn.

Here's Juggin's by Sally Smith Bryant.

Lost! On a Mountain in Maine, by Donn Fendler, William Morrow & Co.

Counting Our Way to Maine, by Maggie Smith

The Story of Sea Glass, by Anne Wescott Dodd

At Home in the Tide Pool, by Alexandra Wright.

The Story of Andre, by Lew Dietz, Down East Books

Newberry - The Life and Times of a Maine Clam, by Vincent Dethier.

Lobsterman, by Dahlov Ipcar, Random House.
The Little Island, by Margaret Wise Brown, Doubleday.
Moose, of Course, by Lynn Plourde, Down East Books.
Cocoa Ice, Diana Appelbaum, Orchard Books.
Puffin's Homecoming: The Story of an Atlantic Puffin, by Soundprints.

For older readers, Sarah Orne Jewett's *The Country of the Pointed Firs* has stood the test of time and *Maine Woods* is Henry David Thoreau's classic account of climbing "Ktaadin". Also for older readers, *She Took to the Woods,* is a biography and selected writings of Louise Dickinson Rich.

For those long car rides, don't overlook some of these Maine titles on audio cassettes. Audio Bookshelf (www.audiobookshelf.com) has several of the above names and all their offerings are unabridged.

Take advantage of the area libraries for borrowing, as a source for Maine literature, and for story hours and crafts workshops (www.public/libraries.com/maine.htm).

Call the South Portland Library Dial-a-Story line (207-767-8162) and have your child listen to a 5 to 8 minute recording of a story read by the children's librarian.

Portland Public Library
207-871-1707
www.portlandlibrary.com
All residents of York and Cumberland County and all students attending local schools may borrow for free.
5 Monument Square, Portland
377 Stevens Avenue, Portland
44 Moody Street, Portland

Portland Public Library continued:
129 Island Avenue, Peaks Island
1600 Forest Avenue, Portland

South Portland Library
482 Broadway, South Portland
155 Wescott Road, South Portland
207-767-7660
www.southportlandlibrary.com

Warren Memorial Library
479 Main Street, Westbrook
207-854-5891

Walker Memorial Library
800 Main Street, Westbrook
207-854-0630

Falmouth Memorial Library
5 Lunt Road, Falmouth
207-781-2351
www.falmouth.lib.me.us

Thomas Memorial Library
6 Scott Dyer Road, Cape Elizabeth
207-799-1720

State Parks & Other Open Spaces

There are four state parks (Crescent Beach, Ferry Beach, Two Lights and Wolfe's Neck Woods) within an easy drive of Portland, and they each have much to recommend them. If you want the brochure *State Parks, Public Reserved Lands, State Historic Sites, Boat Access Sites, Snowmobile Trails, and All-Terrain Vehicle Trails*, call or write to the Bureau of Parks and Lands:

Maine Bureau of Parks and Lands
22 State House Station, Augusta, ME 04333
Telephone: 207- 287-3821
www.maine.gov/doc/parks

If you are willing to drive a little further, still more lovely state parks abound. Popham Beach State Park and Reid State Park together comprise over 1,000 acres.

Campsite reservations can be made online or by phone with Visa or MasterCard (207-287-2209), Monday through Friday. You can also make reservations by mail using check or money order. Send requests to the attention of Reservation Clerk, Parks and Recreations, at the above address.

■AGAMENTICUS WILDERNESS RESERVE

Parks and Recreation Department, York
Riding stable: 207-361-2840
Summit Cycle Shop: 207-363-0470
Open year-round

Located just seven miles from downtown York, this area is the largest contiguous forested area along the entire Atlantic coastal plain. Committed to preservation in the late 1970s, this land encompasses a 32-square mile area around three major hills.

A full-service riding stable is open daily, Memorial Day through Columbus Day, and offers everything from children's lessons to scenic trail rides.

Mountain bikers will find miles of trails, and bike rentals are available at the Summit Cycle Shop. Guided mountain bike tours are a daily option or you can obtain a trail map for exploring on your own.

A BBQ pit, hiking trails, picnic tables, volleyball, and horse shoes are available as well as a comfortable lodge.

In the winter, hikers and cross-country skiers make good use of these lands that are still considered sacred by Native Americans.

■BACK COVE PATHWAY

Baxter Boulevard, Portland

This 3.5 mile pathway cuts around Portland's Back Cove and is the city's most popular recreational facility. Park in the main lot across from Shop'n Save Plaza. Most of the pathway parallels Baxter Boulevard with views looking across the marshes to the city skyline. Come here to walk, bike, roller blade, and even windsurf. (There is enough water 2 ½ hours before and after high tides.) Exercise checkpoints, benches, and a drinking fountain are located along the way. The trail connects to the Eastern Promenade Trail under Tukey's Bridge.

■BATES-MORSE MOUNTAIN CONSERVATION AREA

Morse Mountain Road, Phippsburg
Preserve's office at Bates College: 207-786-6078
Open sunrise to sunset

This 600-acre preserve, just south of Bath, sits on the tip of the Phippsburg peninsula. Take this fairly easy 2-mile hike and you'll pass marshes, beaches, woodlands, meadows and dunes.

Parking is limited to 40 cars, so you could be turned away during the summer months. No dogs or bicycles allowed.

From Portland, drive north on I-295 to I-95 and take exit 28 (Coastal Route 1). Follow Route 1 north into Bath and take a left onto Route 209 (Phippsburg). Stay on Route 209 for 11 miles. Take Route 216 south for 2 miles. Morse Mountain Road will be on the left. The preserve is almost 50 miles from Portland.

■BRADBURY MOUNTAIN STATE PARK
Route 9, Hallowell Road, Pownal
207-688-4712
www.stateparks.com/bradbury_mountain.html
Open year-round
Admission fee

Take the easy quarter mile hike on the Summit Trail to the top of this 460-foot mountain and you will be rewarded with lovely views of Casco Bay. This 590-acre park off Route 9 has six miles of hiking trails, a playground, restrooms, a picnic area, swings, teeters and a horseshoe pit. It is open all year and is a great spot for cross-country skiing and snowshoeing. This is the only state park in southern Maine to offer shared-use trails for horseback riders, mountain bikers, and snowmobilers. Snowshoe rentals are available.

Take I-295 north to exit 22 and follow signs to Bradbury Mountain.

■COFFIN POND
River Road, Brunswick
207-725-6656
www.brunswickme.org/parkrec/coffinpond.htm

Located off Pleasant Street, this is a great place for the whole family, but especially the little ones. Coffin Pond is a chlorinated outdoor pond with lifeguards. A little action is provided by the 55-foot long water slide. A snack bar, restrooms, changing facilities and a picnic area are available. Coffin Pond is owned by the Town of Brunswick.

■CRESCENT BEACH STATE PARK
Route 77, Cape Elizabeth
207-799-5871
Open Memorial Day to Columbus Day
Admission charged

This 4,000-foot sand beach offers gentle surf for swimming. You'll find a snack bar, picnic tables and grills, a children's playground, bike racks, bathrooms, lifeguards, and a bath house with cold water showers. While there is a large parking area available, on hot summer weekends the spaces can get filled up by late morning and you may have to wait for someone to leave before you can get in.

■DEERING OAKS
Forest Avenue, Portland

Designed by Frederick Law Olmstead, this 51-acre city park is a nice place to come and feed the ducks or swans in its large pond, toss a Frisbee, skate, cross-country ski or bike. Portlanders come here for tennis, horse shoes, basketball, softball and the playgrounds. The park was the site of one of the fiercest battles fought in the French and Indian wars.

During the summer, concerts are presented and children's performances are held on scheduled afternoons.

Free parking and public restrooms are available next to the Castle building.

■DESERT OF MAINE

95 Desert Road, Freeport
207-865-6962
www.desertofmaine.com
Open daily, May through mid-October, 9:00 a.m. to dusk
Admission fee charged

In the early nineteenth century this was the home of the Tuttle Farm located on an ancient glacial sand deposit. The topsoil eroded following years of farming and tree cutting until the sand began to take over the farm. A small area of sand in 1897 grew to this fifty-acre desert today. Surrounded by lush forests it is a remarkable sight.

A narrated safari coach gives tours every half hour of the giant sand dunes and nature trails. There is also a museum and a large gift shop. Kids will enjoy the sand designing crafts and a gem stone hunt. The Desert of Maine is recommended by the AAA.

It is located 2 miles from exit 20 off Route 295.

■DUNDEE PARK

Presumpscot Road, Windham
207-893-2415
Open weekends only May 22-June 12;
daily June 17-Labor Day; 8:00 a.m. to sunset
Admission: Windham residents $2.00; children $.50;
non-residents $3.00; children $1.00

Dundee Park consists of a sandy beach and picnic area located along the Presumpscot River. There is a float for jumping

and diving, lifeguards, paddle boats and canoe rentals.
Take Route 302 to River Road to Presumpscot Road.

■EASTERN PROM TRAIL
Cutter Street, Portland
207-775-2411

This waterfront trail is built along an old rail corridor and is part of a planned 30-mile network of trails connecting Portland's shorelines and parks. It runs between East End Beach and the Casco Bay Ferry Terminal. There are two parallel paths; one for walkers and runners, the other a paved one for bikers, skaters and wheelchairs. This oceanfront walkway has scenic island views, benches and picnic tables located along the route.

■FERRY BEACH STATE PARK
Bay View Road, Saco
Park season: 207-283-0067
Off-season: 207-624-6080
Open Memorial Day through Labor Day
Admission charged

Miles of white sand beaches between the Saco River and Pine Point make this an idyllic swimming area for children. A changing room, picnic area, nature trails, and guided nature programs are available. Parking is available for 120 cars and lifeguards are on duty during the summer season.

■FORE RIVER SANCTUARY
Portland
To enter at the west end, turn south off Brighton Avenue on to Rowe Avenue. To enter at the east end, park in the Maine Orthopedics lot at 1601 Congress Street.
Open daily, dawn to dusk

This 85-acre preserve owned by Maine Audubon Society offers up 2.5 miles of trails that let you forget you are within city limits. Hike along a former canal towpath that leads you over the historic Cumberland and Oxford Canal, the Stroudwater salt marsh and eventually to Jewell's Falls, Portland's only natural waterfall. These are all fairly easy walks.
No bikes, ATV's or pets allowed here.

■FORT McCLARY STATE HISTORIC PARK
Pepperrell Road, Route 103, Kittery
Open Memorial Day through Labor Day
Summer: 207-384-5160
Admission: $1.00 per person

Fort McClary was built to protect Maine settlers from enforcement of taxes levied by New Hampshire. Children now spend hours playing in and around this old fort. Built on 27 acres, the park has picnic benches, grills, swings, parking and lovely views across the broad channel of Portsmouth Harbor toward New Hampshire.

■GILSLAND FARM
(Maine Audubon Society Headquarters)
118 Old Route 1, Falmouth
207-781-2330
www.maineaudubon.org
Open year-round, dawn to dusk
Free admission

Depending on the season, join guides for nature walks, go on an amphibian egg hunt at Easter, make and fly your own kite, star gaze or join one of the many programs offered at this lovely spot.

There are more craft projects, Discovery Times, and fun kid offerings here than we can list. Definitely call and get their schedule to take advantage of this great community resource.

The Nature Store is a well-stocked shop for all levels of books, field guides and gift items. The shop is open Monday through Saturday, 9:00 a.m. to 5:00 p.m.

■KID'S WORLD / MAZE CRAZE
Lunt Road, Falmouth

Kid's World playground, located at the Plummer-Motz Elementary School, was specifically built to be handicapped-accessible. It has ground covers that are wheelchair-friendly, lower structures that are reachable from a wheelchair and ramps and platforms instead of stairs and ladders. Located across the schoolyard from the Maze Craze, both playgrounds are located near the intersection of Lunt Road and Route 9.

Maze Craze is very popular with local children. Kids disappear into one end of the playground and reappear at the opposite end. A double-decker sandbox sits in the middle.

■LAUDHOLM FARM
342 Laudholm Farm Road, Wells
207-646-1555
www.wellsreserve.org
Open year-round. Trails are open 8:00 a.m. to 5:00 p.m. daily
Admission fee charged

This historic 1,600-acre salt water farm has been owned by the nonprofit Laudholm Trust since 1986. The property has seven miles of trails that cover diverse ecosystems and the farm has been used for estuarine research since its takeover by the trust. Tours are available starting at the elegant Victorian visitor center and gift shop, or you can explore on your own.

The Wells Reserve at the Farm offers an extensive and easy trail system through 1,600 acres of fields, forest and coast. Ask about their family tours and their children's programs which are offered several times a month.

The Discovery Tours offer 10 different self-guided tours of the preserve. Illustrated booklets ($5.00 each) are full of activities and information. Children can also borrow one of the farm's backpacks that come stocked with binoculars, a compass and field guides for use on the tour.

There are many children's programs and special events scheduled throughout the year.

■MARGINAL WAY
Route 1, Perkins Cove, Ogunquit
207-646-2939

Park down by Perkins Cove and stroll this famously scenic walk along the rocky coastline.

Marginal Way begins by Oarweed Restaurant & Lobster Pound (207-646-4022) and ends a little more than a mile later with a beacon marking the path. This is an easy walk for youngsters, just take care if you wander off the pathway and down onto the cliffs. Near the water the rocks are very slippery and there is a strong undertow.

■MAST LANDING SANCTUARY
Upper Mast Landing Road, Freeport
(off Bow Street and Flying Point Road)
207-781-2330
Open year-round
Admission free

This Audubon Sanctuary offers 3.5 miles of trails that wind along a tidal river, fields, forests and streams. With 140 acres of meadows and orchards this is also a great property in the winter for cross-country skiing and sledding. No bikes are allowed on the trails.

A hike along the Loop Trail is only about a mile and a half and is flat most of the way.

■POPHAM BEACH STATE PARK

Route 209, 10 Perkins Farm Lane, Phippsburg
General Information: 207-389-1335
Current tide and parking information: 207-389-9125
www.maine.gov/doc/parks
Open year-round, dawn to dusk
Admission mid-April to mid-October; adults $3; children $1

Popham Beach State Park spreads over 529-acres and one of the loveliest beaches in the state. When the kids get tired of playing on the sandy beach and in the tidal pools, you can head 2 miles further down Route 209 and investigate the ruins of the nineteenth-century Fort Popham where the English first tried to colonize New England.

You'll find picnicking, fishing, bathhouses and even showers. The park is located 15 miles from Bath.

■PORTLAND HEAD LIGHT AND MUSEUM AND FORT WILLIAMS PARK

1000 Shore Road, Cape Elizabeth
207-799-2661 or 207-799-5251
www.portlandheadlight.com
Park open year-round, dawn to dusk; museum open June - October, 10 a.m.-4 p.m.; Nov., Dec., and May, weekends only. Admission to the park is free. To the museum: Adults $2, children $1, under 6 free

Built in 1791, this is Maine's oldest and most photographed lighthouse. Located in Fort Williams this beautiful, seaside park is owned by the town of Cape Elizabeth. The light marks the entrance to Portland Harbor, and the surrounding grounds boast sprawling, grassy lawns, breathtaking ocean vistas and lots of picnic areas. There is a pretty little beach for swimming, but bring your water socks as it is fairly rocky. The town-owned museum, located in the former keeper's quarters, highlights the history of lighthouses and navigation.

But don't go to Portland Head Light just to see the magnificent lighthouse, because Fort Williams itself, built in 1873 to guard the entrance to Casco Bay, is worth the trip. The stone remains of Goddard Mansion seem to spark kids' imaginations and prompt many games of hide and seek, pirates and explorers.

■PORTLAND TRAILS
One India Street, Portland
207-775-2411
www.trails.org

Portland Trails is an urban conservation organization whose goal is to create a 30-mile network of recreational trails within Greater Portland. They have a beautiful, four-color map that shows biking and walking trails, city parks, public open spaces, and points of interest for Portland, Falmouth, Westbrook and South Portland that they sell for $4.95.

Most book stores in Portland carry the guide or you can purchase it online at their website.

■PRATT'S BROOK PARK
Two entrances: Meadow Way and North Road, Yarmouth
207-846-2406

This 200-acre park is designated for passive recreational use so it is a fine spot for hiking and cross-country skiing.

The ski trails are maintained and groomed. A map and trail guide is available which classifies trails as easier, more difficult and most difficult.

■REID STATE PARK
375 Seguinland Road, Rt. 127, Georgetown
207-371-2303
www.maine.gov/doc/parks/
Open year-round, 9:00 a.m. to sunset
Admission: Adults $3.50; children $1.00; under 5 free

One of the most popular swimming areas along this part of the coast is 14 miles south of Bath and about an hour and 15 minutes from Portland. More than a mile of sandy beach with lovely island vistas awaits visitors to Reid. The 766-acre park has lots of sand dunes, salt marshes, ledges, sandy beaches and even a salt-water lagoon to wander around. Two sandy beaches are great for swimming and fishing. They have bathhouses, showers and a snack bar. Lifeguards are on duty in summer months.

■ROYAL RIVER PARK
East Elm Street, Yarmouth
207-846-2406

This quiet little 20-acre park sits between two falls. It has wooded picnic areas, a fish ladder and a parking area. A one-mile paved walkway runs along the river past some rapids and is a nice walk or bike ride.

When it's cold enough for long enough, the Royal Rive freezes over and is used for skating and cross-country skiing.

■SACO HEATH PRESERVE
Route 112, Saco
www.sacobaytrails.org/heath.shtm
Open sunrise to sunset. Pets are not permitted.

Located on over 500 acres, a trail leads through the forest to a 2,300-foot boardwalk that crosses the peat bog.

The boardwalk also passes over a lake that was left when the last glacier passed over the area 9,000 years ago.

The trail is reached by driving northwest on the Buxton Road (Route 112) for 1.7 miles after passing over the Maine Turnpike. The parking lot, located behind a row of tress is marked with a Nature Conservancy sign.

■SCARBOROUGH BEACH STATE PARK
Black Point Road (Route 207), Scarborough
207-883-2416
Open April 1 to Labor Day
Admission fee charged

This is a pretty little 5-acre park that has a sandy beach for swimming, as well as marshes and dunes. Locals can be found fishing here. Surfers like this beach for it waves and unrestricted hours when surfing is allowed. There are changing rooms, lifeguards and parking.

■SCARBOROUGH MARSH NATURE CENTER
Route 9, Pine Point Road, Scarborough
207-883-5100 or 207-781-2330
Open mid-May through mid-June, Saturdays only.
Mid-June to Labor Day, daily, 9:30 a.m. to 5:30 p.m.

This is the largest salt marsh in the state, covering 3,100 acres of tidal marsh, salt creeks, fresh marsh, and uplands.
    There is a regular schedule of nature education programs as well as a self-guided nature trail, indoor exhibits, and a nature store with many field guides, children's environmental toys and books, t-shirts and more.
    Programs include canoe tours and rentals, nature art, pottery, story hours, nature photography and bug hunts. Don't forget the bug spray.

■SEBAGO LAKE STATE PARK

11 Park Access Road, Casco
Park season: 207-693-6613   Off-season: 207-693-6231
www.state.me.us/cgi-bin/doc/parks
Open May 15- October 1
Admission fee charged

This forested lakeside park with its warm sandy beach is located on the lake's north shore and boasts shady picnic areas, a snack bar, campground and lifeguards. The park's 1,400 acres feature woodlands, ponds and bogs as well as the extensive swimming beach.

Located between Naples and South Casco, the crystal waters of Sebago Lake provide Portland's water supply. There are also bathhouses, showers and a boat ramp.

■STEVE POWELL WILDLIFE MANAGEMENT AREA

Swan Island (on the Kennebec River)
Contact: Maine Dept. of Inland Fisheries and Wildlife
284 State Street, Augusta
207-547-5322
www.state.me.us/ifw
Open first day of May through the end of September.
Reservations accepted on a first-come, first-served basis for both day and camping uses

Located in Merrymeeting Bay, this unique wildlife area is made up of two islands and several hundred acres of adjoining tidal flats. All access, both for day use and camping, is by reservations and written permit only. The Department of Inland Fisheries provides transportation to and from the island. Swan Island is better known than Little Swan Island and is available for camping with special programs for visitors. It is 4 miles long with a gravel road and nature trails. This is a game preserve and you are likely to see nesting bald eagles and white-tailed deer. A self-guided tour is available, taking visitors from one end of the island to the other. The island has been listed on the National Register of Historic Places and there are 38 historical houses and sites to visit.

The Abernaki Indians first inhabited this area and called the island "Swango" (Island of Eagles). They were followed by the white settlers in 1607. Eventually colonists began to settle on Swan Island despite continued problems with the Native Americans.

The very complete self-guiding tour booklet also features illustrations of animal tracks in the back so your child can be a nature detective and discern whether you have crossed paths with a coyote, ruffled grouse, wild turkey or deer. You will not need to worry about crowds, there is a maximum of 60 visitors allowed on the island at any one time. Swan Island is about 50 miles north of Portland.

■THOMAS POINT BEACH
Route 24, Cook's Corner, Brunswick
207-725-6009 or 877-TPB-4321
www.thomaspointbeach.com
Open mid-May to Labor Day, daily, 9:00 a.m. to sunset
Admission: Adults $3.50; under 12 $2.00; under 3 free

As if a clean, sandy beach on tidal water overlooking Thomas Bay weren't enough, add to this lifeguards, a snack bar, gift shop, arcade, ice cream parlor, special events throughout the summer, a large playground, 64-acres of beautiful lawns and picnic groves, volleyball, softball and horseshoe areas as well as 500- plus picnic tables and hot showers. Phew! The sandy beach is on a tidal water though, so low tide can reveal mud flats.

■TWO LIGHTS STATE PARK
66 Two Lights Road, Cape Elizabeth
Open year-round

Two Lights features a picturesque walkway with gorgeous views spread out over 40 acres on a site that once served as a World War II coastal defense installation. Picnic tables and grills are available. There is no swimming beach here but I have it on good authority that some tasty striped bass and a bluefish or two have been caught off the rocks. Of the two lights that give the park its name, only the eastern lighthouse operates today. The western lighthouse is no longer in use and is privately owned.

If you continue about a mile further on the Two Lights Road, you will come to The Lobster Shack (207-799-1677). You can order some great seafood (best lobster rolls in town) and eat it at their picnic tables overlooking the rockbound coast or inside the informal restaurant. Crescent Beach State Park with its long sandy beach is only a half mile away.

■VAUGHAN WOODS STATE PARK
Route 236, South Berwick
Contact: Dept. of Conservation: 207-693-6231

Located on the banks of the Salmon Falls River, this 250-acre park offers a picnic area and nature trails that accommodate hikers in the summer and cross-country skiers in winter. The first cows in Maine landed here in the 1600s.

■WINSLOW MEMORIAL PARK
Staples Point Road, South Freeport
207-865-4198
Open Memorial Day to October
Admission fee charged

Leave the hubbub of Freeport shopping and stop at this 90-acre municipal park for a rest at the picnic area, a walk along the sandy beach, or a hike on the nature trail that meanders around the park perimeter. It is one of the warmest saltwater beaches in Maine. But check your tide chart, as at low tide some areas are muddy.

From downtown Freeport, take Bow Street to South Freeport Road. Three miles later Staples Point Road will be on the left. Follow signs to Winslow Park. Or from Route1, turn onto South Freeport Toad at the Big Indian. Turn right onto Staples Point Road and the park is located at the end.

■WOLFE'S NECK WOODS STATE PARK

425 Wolfe's Neck Road, Freeport
April through October: 207-865-4465
Off-season: 207-865-6080
www.state.me.us/doc/parks
Open year-round
Admission charged April through October

Founded by Mr. & Mrs. L.M.C. Smith, advocates of non-pesticide agriculture, Wolfe's Neck stretches magnificently over 230 acres of forest and shoreline just four and a half miles from L.L. Bean.

Here you can hike along trails marked with interpretive signs and use the picnic tables and charcoal grills. The views along the five miles of hiking trails are lovely as the path weaves through the woods and along the shores of Casco Bay and the Harraseeket River. Keep an eye out for Googins Island and see if the kids can spot the osprey nest.

The park features the state's first nature trail designed to accommodate people in wheelchairs.

A daily guided nature walk is offered during July and August.

Across from L.L. Bean, turn onto Bow Street and follow for 2.4 miles to Wolfe's Neck Road. Continue for two miles, the park will be on your right.

Room for Notes

"Pick Your Own" Orchards & Farms

PICK YOUR OWN FRUIT: BERRIES

Mid-June to late-July, Maine has lots of farms that let you and your children come and pick your own strawberries. Don't forget to call first to be sure they are picking the day you want to go. Come August, start picking blueberries! To check out more complete listings, visit www.mainefoodandfarms.com.

Alewive's Brook Farm
83 Old Ocean House Road, Cape Elizabeth
207-799-8894
(strawberries)

Dearodad
14 Grover Lane, Brunswick
207-725-7028
(strawberries, wild blueberries, apples, raspberries)

Jordan's Farm
21 Wells Road, Cape Elizabeth
207-799-1466
www.jordansfarm.com
(strawberries and flowers)

Maxwell's Farm
Two Lights Road, Cape Elizabeth
207-799-3383
www.maxwellsfarm.com
(strawberries, flowers, pumpkins)

Patten's Farm
269 County Road (Rte.22), Gorham
207-839-4667
www.pattensberryfarm.com
(strawberries)

Spiller Farm
1123 Branch Road, Wells
207-985-2575
(strawberries, raspberries, blueberries, apples)

Stewart's Farm
Rte. 1A in Stockton Springs, Portland
207-879-1667
(strawberries)

APPLE ORCHARDS

Maine's unique combination of climate, soil and terrain produces the world's finest Macintosh apples and many other favorites. October is apple-picking time in Maine and the following come-pick-your-own orchards make for an invigorating autumn event. Did you know that Maine cider is as high in Vitamin C as any citrus juice?

Douglas Hill Orchard
Orchard Road, Sebago
207-787-2745
(apples and pumpkins)

Intervale Farm
752 Mayall Road, New Gloucester
207-926-3008
(apples)

Moulton Orchards
Route 35, Standish
207-225-3455
(apples)

Randall Orchard
Randall Road (off Rte. 25), Standish
207-642-3500
(apples, pumpkins, gourds)

Romac Orchard
H Road, Sanford
207-636-3247
(apples, hay rides)

MAPLE SUGARING

In late February, March and April when the sap starts to run, maple sugaring is an event in Maine. Children are always amazed to know that the sap they see dripping from the trees is the same stuff they pour on their Sunday pancakes.

Did you know that the average maple tree isn't tapped until it is almost forty years old?

All Maine maple syrup commercially sold is Grade A quality and then it is further classified by its flavor and color characteristics as light, medium, dark and extra dark. Extra dark amber, with its hearty flavor, is the most requested syrup grade.

The fourth Sunday in March the state celebrates Maine Maple Day and many sugarhouses are open to the public (hint: wear boots).

Cooper's Maple Products
81 Chute Road, Windham
207-892-7276

Grandpa Joe's Sugar House
103 Murch road, Baldwin
207-787-2903

Green Maple Farm
77 Bridgton Road, East Sebago
207-787-2424

Merrifield Farms
195 North Gorham Road, Gorham
207-892-5061

Nash Valley Farm
Nash Road, Windham
207-892-7019

Parsons Maple Products
316 Buck Street, Gorham
207-839-4466

Pumpkin Hill Sugar House
12 Pumpkin Hill Road, Gorham
207-892-9387

Snell Family Farm
Rte. 112,   Bar Mills
207-929-6166
www.snellfamilyfarm.com

Sweet William's
Route 11, Casco
207-627-7362

CORN MAZES

In the fall, when the corn stalks are eight-feet tall, some farms create winding, twisting mazes with dead ends, and secret rooms. Most of these farms also offer pumpkins, cider and other activities.

Chipman Farm's Pumpkin Land
Range Hill Road, Poland Spring
Pumpkin Land Hotline: 207-998-2027
www.chipmanpumpkinland.com
Open every weekend October 1 through October 31
A corn maze, 60-foot slide, farm theme games and haunted hayrides all await your family about 35 miles north of Portland. A horse-drawn carriage carries you to the pumpkin patch.

Pumpkin Valley Farm
Union Falls Road
Dayton
207-929-4545
www.pumpkinvalleyfarm.com
Every year this farm creates an incredible, 5-acre corn maze. They also offer an animal barnyard, cow train, slide tunnel and a Corn Launcher ($1.00 per person) among other activities. The last weekend they are open you can travel the maze by the moonlight (or flashlight) from 6:00 p.m. to 9:00 p.m.

From the Maine Turnpike take exit 32 (Biddeford) and turn right onto Route 111. Turn right onto Route 35. At the intersection of Route 35 & Route 5 - go straight. Take an immediate right onto Hight Road. At the stop sign, go straight onto Union Falls Road. Follow to the end. Dayton is about 28 miles southwest of Portland.

Zach's Farm
7 Colby Turner Road, York
207-363-4502
"The Great Corn Maze" is created every year with lawn mowers and bush cutters carving out designs over 25 acres of cornfields. They deliver you to the field by way of a 20-minute hayride. On the weekends, you can play "flashlight tag" in the maze from 7:00 p.m. to 10:00 p.m. Hayrides, pick-your-own-pumpkin and more farm activities are offered.

Room for Notes

Happy Campers

There are many resources in your library and online to help you select good summer camps. The Maine Youth Camping Association, P.O. Box 1861, Portland, ME 04104, is an excellent place to start. Call (800-536-7712), write or visit them online (www.mainecamps.org) and request a copy of *Children's Summer Camps in Maine.* We list here just a few of the unique camps in the area.

See also: The Creative Child,Summer Camp 207-839-3982; and The Brick Store Museum.

■ARTREK
Portland Museum of Art, Education Department
Seven Congress Square, Portland
207-775-6148
www.portlandmuseum.org

The Portland Museum of Art's summer day camp for kids ages 6 to 15 takes place at the city's beautiful museum. Children make art together in week-long celebrations of the arts. The Museum's exhibitions serve as inspiration as students work in traditional as well as non-traditional media. All sessions are led by artists/teachers. Special opening celebrations follow each Artrek session. Classes are held Monday through Friday.

■AUDUBON CAMP
20 Gilsland Farm Road, Falmouth
207-781-2330
www.maineaudubon.org

Maine Audubon offers summer camp programs in Falmouth, Freeport and at historic Hog Island Audubon Camp, a 330-acre island in Muscongus Bay.

Summer day camps offer ages 6-13 one- and two-week sessions where they explore the natural world.
Overnight youth camp at Hog Island off mid-coast Maine gives children ages 11-13 a full week to learn about nature.
Overnight camp for teens at Hog Island offers one-of-a-kind adventures to small groups of teens ages 14-17.
Preschool Discovery Programs throughout the year for children ages 2-5 include their popular preschool summer programs.

■CAMP KETCHA
Camp Fire Boys and Girls, Hitinowa Council
336 Black Point Road, Scarborough
207-883-8977
www.campketcha.com

Camp Ketcha is a non-profit, co-ed day camp for children ages 4 through 15. It is located on 133 acres of wooded land with a pond, swimming pool, adventure ropes course and equestrian center.

■CAMP SUNSHINE
35 Acadia Road, Casco
207-655-3800
www.campsunshine.org

Founded in 1984, this non-profit, year-round retreat offers support and joy to children with life-threatening illnesses and their immediate families. At this very special spot families have a chance to swim, boat, create arts and crafts, fish, play mini-golf and much more.

■CHILDREN'S MUSEUM OF MAINE
142 Free Street, Portland
207-828-1234
www.kitetails.com
Prices vary, registration required

The Museum's camps are designed for children ages 4 to 11, with half-day camps for young ones and full-day camps for older children. Their camps are generally focused on science and multicultural topics, and many include trips to local parks, beaches and other area attractions.

Casco Bay Environmental Camp takes kids (ages 8-11) aboard a real schooner to investigate the ecology of the coast and the physics of sailing.

Stage Stories turns familiar stories into plays with props and costumes that kids (ages 4-6) design themselves.

Call or check out their web site for a schedule of all the great camps that are offered.

■CHILDREN'S THEATER OF MAINE
317 Marginal Way, Portland
207-878-2774

This popular theater runs four different summer camps in Creative Arts for ages 4 to 10 and The Jester's Troupe for ages 11 to 14. One of the oldest children's theaters in the country, they run the camp mid-July through mid-August. The CT has been looking for a new home and as we go to print they are close to purchasing an armory in South Portland.

■MAINE COLLEGE OF ART
97 Spring Street, Portland
207-775-3052
www.meca.edu

MECA, as it is called locally, moved into the old Porteous Mitchell store building at 522 Congress Street and turned it into a state-of-the-art studio facility. They offer a variety of Young Arts Programs for kids ages 6 through 12. Check online or request a catalogue to read about their programs in Ceramics, Beginning Photography, Painting and much more.

■THE MORRIS FARM SUMMER DAY CAMP
Rt. 27, Gardiner Road, Wiscassett
207-882-4080
www.morrisfarm.org

The Morris Farm is a 60-acre working organic dairy farm that is home to rolling fields and a pond, waterfall, barn and farmhouse.

Each camp day is filled with folk crafts, farm animal care, organic gardening and ecology games.

The farm offers six one-week sessions for children ages 6 to 11.

■MUSEUM OF AFRICAN CULTURE
122 Spring Street, Portland
207-871-7188
www.tribalartmuseum.com/programs.htm

Discover Africa Camp is a five-day program offering art and multi-cultural programs for ages 4 through 14. Four two-week sessions are held Monday through Friday from 8:30 a.m. to 3:00 p.m.

The program explores African art and culture through mask making, painting, story telling, literature, drama and language, African music and dance.

■OLD YORK HISTORICAL SOCIETY
207 York Street, York
207-363-4974
www.oldyork.org

The Society offers a one-week long camp in July. Designed for children ages 8 through 12, activities introduce children to what life was like in the 18th century through a series of hands-on activities.

They offer several children's programs throughout the year so check their website for all the latest listings.

■PORTLAND CONSERVATORY OF MUSIC
116 Free Street, Portland
207-775-3356
www.portlandconservatory.com

The conservatory offers multiple week-long summer day camps in all areas of music such as jazz camp, flute camp, rock and roll camp, piano and string camp.

Most of the camp offerings here have about 10 students. The rock and roll camp can easily have three times that number, so apply early if this is the session your looking for. The idea is to show participants how to create garage bands and then go forward to record and promote a CD.

■PORTLAND SYMPHONY ORCHESTRA MUSIC CAMP
Congress Street, Portland
207-773-6128
www.portlandsymphony.com/education

Free to concert-ticket holders, the PSO Music Camp is geared to children ages nine and up and includes interactive pre-concert activities such as puzzles, composer games, and a backstage tour. Camp precedes the Sunday Classical Concert and begins at 1:50 p.m., the concert begins at 2:30 p.m.

■RIPPLEFFECT
P.O. Box 441, Portland
207-791-7870
www.rippleffect.net

Rippleffect "promotes development through learning adventures in living classrooms." The organization specializes in adventure and wilderness experiences that build confidence and self-esteem while exploring the beauty of the Maine coast. Part of the experience is kayaking around Casco Bay and experiencing camp on the organization's own Cow Island.

■WESTERLY WINDS GOLF COURSE
& SPORTS PARK
853 Cumberland Street (River Road), Westbrook
207-854-9463
www.westerlywinds.com/summercamps.htm

Westerly Winds offers several week-long tennis or golf camps for kids ages 8 through 14. Held on the 250-acre property, children also participate in baseball, softball, basketball, volleyball and shuffleboard as well as enjoying the Westerly Winds swimming pool.

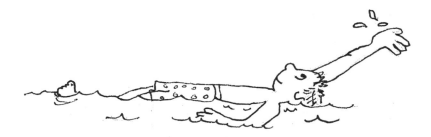

■WOLFE'S NECK FARM
184 Barnett Road, Freeport
207-865-4363
www.wolfesneckfarm.org

Summer Day Camp offers hands-on, outdoor learning that focuses on farms, gardens, forest and wetland ecosystems, and healthy living, as well as arts and theater for children ages 4 through 14.

■YMCA and YWCA CAMPS
Check with your local Y as they offer a variety of camping opportunities.
 ■70 Forest Avenue, Portland
 207-874-1111
 ■14 Old South Freeport Road, Freeport
 207-865-9600
 ■87 Spring Street, Portland
 207-874-1130

Sports

Located on the ocean, with lakes, ponds, rivers and mountains all an easy drive away, Portland is a haven for sports of all kinds and seasons.

The city also enjoys two professional sports teams, The Portland Pirates hockey team and The Portland Sea Dogs baseball team.

L.L. Bean Outdoor Discovery School
95 Main Street, Freeport
888-552-3261
www.llbean.com/ods
Open year-round, 24 hours a day
The famous retailer offers such a wide variety of workshops and "Walk-On Adventures" that it is impossible to fit it under just one category, so we are giving it a spot all its own. From April through November they have workshops in archery, fly-fishing, day targeting, wilderness training, kayaking, canoeing and outdoor photography.

November to March their Winter Sports School has classes in cross-country skiing, snowshoeing, winter camping and outdoor photography.

Sign up in advance or go to the retail store in Freeport to check into the "Walk-On Adventures" where you can learn the basics of a new sport in an hour and a half to two hours. Classes are first-come, first-serve, cost $12 per person and all necessary equipment is provided.

PROFESSIONAL SPECTATOR SPORTS

★Portland Pirates
531 Congress Street, Portland
207-828-4665
www.portlandpirates.com
Season is October through April
Cumberland County's 6,000-seat Civic Center is home to the
city's hockey team, an affiliate of the AHL Mighty Ducks of
Anaheim. Games are played from fall through spring and the
entertainment between periods helps to keep children
interested.

★Portland Sea Dogs
271 Park Avenue, Portland
800-936-3647 or 207-874-9300
For tickets call: 207-879-9500
www.portlandseadogs.com
Season: April through October
The boys of summer are the Double-A Eastern team affiliate
of the Boston Red Sox and their games are so popular they
tend to sell out a couple of weeks in advance. Portland fans
have embraced the Sea Dogs from the beginning and have
been known to set Eastern League records for total
attendance. All games are played at Hadlock Field, a small
stadium near downtown that while always making
improvements, still has an old-fashioned feel to it. This is a
pleasant venue for a family afternoon or evening. Lots of kid-
oriented entertainment between innings and tasty food make
the Portland Sea Dogs worth the call for tickets.

Fans can park at the Maine Medical Center Parking Garage located at 887 Congress Street or at various temporary lots set up by area businesses located around Hadlock Field. The parking lot next to Hadlock Field is for handicapped parking only prior to and during the games.

BIKING

With its breathtaking views and cooling coastal breezes, Portland and the surrounding area are ideal locations for bicycling enthusiasts. Free information on biking trails is available from the Maine Publicity Bureau (207-846-0833). Also, the Convention and Visitors Bureau has suggestions (207-772-9800).

An excellent source is **Portland Trails** (207-775-2411), an urban conservation organization whose goal is to create a 30-mile network of recreational trails within Greater Portland. They sell an excellent, clearly drawn color map that prominently features all the biking trails. Visit their website: www.trails.org.

★Androscoggin River Bicycle Path
Grover Lane, Brunswick
207-725-6656
Open dawn to dusk
This 2.5 mile-long paved path runs along the river between Grover Lane and Water Street. Lined on one side with the river and on the other with plenty of trees, granite benches, restrooms and separate lanes for cyclists and pedestrians.

★Hinckley Park
Highland Avenue, South Portland
This is a favorite spot for mountain biking. For more mountain bike friendly spots contact **The New England Mountain Bike Association** (800-576-3622) or visit their website (www.nemba.org/ridingzone/places-me.html).

A few recommended easy trails in Portland:
Peaks Island - 4- mile loop, paved road
Back Cove Trail - 3.5- mile loop, shared use
Eastern Prom Trail (East End Beach) - 2.1 mile, shared use

CANOEING & KAYAKING

Interest in sea kayaking along Maine's miles of rocky coastline has exploded in the last 20 years. The state is home to the nation's first long-distance "water-trail", established in 1987. It winds 325 miles along the coast from Portland to Machias and visits over 70 state and privately owned islands along the way. You must be a member of the **Maine Island Trail Association** in Portland (207-761-8225), a private non-profit organization, to gain permission to visit many of these islands and to receive the guidebook, published annually, that describes the sea trail and the islands it incorporates. Visit them on the web: www.mita.org.

If you feel confident to go off on your own, the following spots are relatively easy excursions:
The **Harraseeket River**, Freeport
Launch from Mast Landing (see page 115)

Salmon Falls River, South Berwick
Launch from Vaughan Woods State Park(see page 124)
Great Falls Boat Launch, Windham
Launch from small parking area on Windham Center Road.
The Presumpscot River runs through Windham, Gorham,
Westbrook, Falmouth and Portland. You can also launch
from Dundee Park (see page 110). Visit the Friends of the
Presumpscot River's website for more information about the
river (www.presumpscotriver.org).

For a little more guidance and equipment rental, try one of the
following spots:

★Dragonworks Inc.
Stevens Road, Bowdoinham
207-666-8481
Kayaking instruction, boats and tours

★Gone With the Wind
524 Pool Road, Biddeford
207-283-8446
Kayak eco-tours, windsurfing, sales and rentals

★Into the Wild Expeditions
North Yarmouth
207-829-0940
Canoe and sea kayak adventures, instruction and eco-tours

★Maine Island Kayak Co.
70 Luther Street, Peaks Island
207-766-2373 or 800-796-2373
www.maineislandkayak.com
This is one of the oldest and most respected organizations with professional guides. Since 1986, Maine Island has been offering both touring and instruction. Half-day trips paddle from their base on Peaks Island out to the islands on southern Casco Bay.

MIKCO offers trips designed specifically for you and your children, a chance for families to join together along Maine's coastal islands. A three-day family trip (suitable for ages 10-12) provides families with double kayaks that are easy to pack, stable and allow the parent to do most of the work. From their base on Peaks Island out to the islands in southern Casco Bay. Their Ocean Adventure Kids Camp I and II offer 7-day kayaking camps for children ages 12-16. MIKCO's rustic boathouse is 15 minutes by the Casco Bay Lines ferry from Portland.

★Saco Bound
Route 302, Center Conway, New Hampshire
603-447-2177
www.sacobound.com
May through mid-October, Saco Bound offers complete canoe and Kayak rental programs. This was one of our favorite trips when our children were little. The Saco River is for the most part a clean, gentle, often shallow river that meanders through scenic stretches dotted with small sandy beaches that are perfect to pull up to for a picnic or to stretch your legs.

Once you have rented your equipment, picked up a map and signed in, you simply go to their private launch, park your car, and hop in the waiting kayak or canoe. A gentle current helps you along. An introductory trip is a 3 mile, 1 hour trip to Weston's Bridge.

Even when our children were small we enjoyed the half-day trip to the Pig Farm. It is 6.4 miles and takes from 2 to 3 hours. Pack sandwiches and drinks (no glass bottles) and it makes for a great day. It is busy in the summer months, but if you go when schools are in session, you will have many parts of the river to yourself.

Center Conway is about an hour from Portland.

★Seaspray Kayaking
Old Bath Road, Brunswick
207-443-3646
www.seaspraykayaking.com

Guided tours as well as hourly rental, instruction and sunrise/sunset paddles. Two lakes, the Maine Island Trail, Sheepscot Bay, Casco Bay and the ocean are all accessed from their kayaking centers.

★Scarborough Marsh
Rt. 9, Pine Point Road, Scarborough
207-883-5100
www.maineaudubon.org

This 3,100-acre estuary is operated by Audubon. Park and check in at the Nature Center. From there they operate several educational programs as well as canoe tours, rentals and a boat-launch site. On windy days, the paddling here becomes difficult and Audubon recommends that you paddle out against the tide and then let the tide help bring you back in. Check tide tables at www.maineharbors.com.

CLIMBING

★Maine Rock Gym
127 Marginal Way, Portland
207-780-6370
www.merockgkym.com
Maine Rock is an indoor/outdoor climbing gym with equipment rental and instruction available. Minimum age is six and minimum age to belay (run the ropes) is twelve.

A liability release form must be signed by everyone using the facility and anyone under eighteen must have one signed by their parent/legal guardian.

They have climbing camps, are available for birthday parties and even have a mobile rock wall that can be rented for parties and events.

FISHING

Maine's coastline has many estuaries and bays where you can hook mackerel, pollock, bluefish and striped bass (called stripers). Surf fishing from the beaches is a common sight with people angling for stripers and bluefish.

If you are looking for a place to throw in a line in Portland head down to **Portland's Public Pier**. This site is popular among shore anglers, especially when mackerel are in. Parking is limited though.

Other city spots are the **Eastern Promenade Boat Launch**, located on Cutter Street.

Just over the bridge in South Portland, located off Route 77 and next to Bug Light is the **South Portland Municipal Boat Ramp.**

And **Spring Point Ledge Light,** also off Route 77 and close to the Southern Maine College campus, provides plenty of beach access.

For a list of locations open for public fishing, go to www.maine.gov/dmr/recreational/saltwaterfishing.htm

★**Bailey Island Fishing Tournament**
This granddaddy of all Maine saltwater tournaments has a variety of children's categories. Watch your Portland paper for details. Sponsored by the Casco Bay Tuna Club since 1938, if you enter the tournament you automatically become a member. While you and the kids may not be up for trying to reel in a 550 lb. tuna, for a smaller entrance fee, there is a junior category where kids under age 12 can weigh in bluefish, mackerel and striped bass for prizes.

★**Royal River Striper Tournament**
Yarmouth
Check local listings
Royal River puts on a Kids' Mackerel and Bluefish Tournament every year. The tournament is based at the Royal River Boatyard in Yarmouth and is run by the Yarmouth Rotary Club.

CHARTERED FISHING TRIPS

Maine's ocean ledges hold some of the best ground fishing on the East Coast. A half-day charter, in calm, close- to-shore waters angling for cod, haddock, pollock or monkfish would be perfect for kids. Ask them to bag any fish you catch so it will be ready for the grill or your freezer.

★Bunny Clark Deep Sea Fishing
Perkins Cove Road, Ogunquit
207-646-2214 (offers half-day fishing trips)
www.bunnyclark.com

★Go Fish Charters
78 E Street, South Portland
207-799-1339

★Kristin K Charters
8 Oakdale Street, South Portland
207-749-5540
www.kristinkcharters.com

★Maine Fishing & Diving Charters
175 Harriet Street, South Portland
207-799-9826
www.mainefishin.com

★Olde Port Mariner Fleet
Long Wharf, Portland
207-775-0727 or 1-800-437-3270
www.marinerfleet.com

★Ugly Anne
Perkins Cove Road, Ogunquit
207-646-7202
www.uglyanne.com

GOLF

Most golf courses are open April to November. For miniature golf courses, check the chapter *Amusement Parks & Arcades.* The following are all open to the public, welcome children and many have golf programs and lessons for kids.

★Biddeford-Saco Country Club
101 Old Orchard Road, Saco
207-282-5883

★Golf Learning Center & Practice Park
147 Bruce Hill Road, Cumberland
General Info: 207-829-9116   Toll Free: 877-749-3788
www.cmgolfschool.com
Located on a quiet, secluded setting the Practice Park offers all grass tee lines overlooking eight target greens. There is a 7,500 square foot bent grass putting green. There are pitching, chipping and bunker areas to sharpen your short game skills.

The Learning Center offers top quality instruction from the PGA teaching staff. The Junior Golf School has two to four full days of instruction as well as ½ -day and one-day schools.

Annual memberships and day passes are available.

★Municipal Golf Course
Westbrook Street, South Portland
207-879-6131

★Nonesuch River Golf Club
304 Gorham Road, Scarborough
207-883-0007
www.nonesuchgolf.com
This 203-acre facility features a meticulously maintained 18-hole championship golf course, a modern 2,500 square-foot clubhouse, and a full-size practice range and green.
     Their Golf Academy offers a wide variety of classes for all levels of golfers and they have a Junior Golf Program.

★Out of the Rough Indoor Golf
16 Pomerleau Street, Biddeford
207-284-9900 or www.ootrgolf.com
Eight golf simulators for course or driving range play.

★Pleasant Hill Golf Course
38 Chamberlain Road, Scarborough
207-883-9340

★Riverside Municipal Golf Course
1158 Riverside Street, Portland
207-797-3524   www.ci.portland.me.us/rec.htm
This is Portland's only municipal golf course. Founded in 1935, Riverside is run by the City of Portland Parks and Recreation Department. The North Course is a 6,406 yard par 72. But the South Course is a quaint 9-hole course that is

easily walked and comes with the reputation of a relaxed atmosphere. Check out their Junior Golf Camps.

★Sable Oaks Golf Club
505 Country Club Drive, South Portland
207-775-6257
www.sableoaks.com
Sable Oaks ranked a 3 ½ Star Award in *Golf Digest's* "Places to Play". They offer Junior rates as well as lessons and clinics.

★South Portland Golf Course
155 Wescott Road, South Portland
207-775-0005

★Southern Maintenance Women's Golf
128 Warren Avenue, Portland
207-797-2268

★Twin Falls Golf Club
364 Spring Street, Westbrook
207-854-5397

★Westerly Winds Golf Course
771 Cumberland Street, Westbrook
207-854-9463   (see page 56)

★Willowdale Golf Club
52 Willowdale Road, Scarborough
207-883-9351
www.willowdalegolf.com

HORSEBACK RIDING

★Durgin Farm
1392 North Road, North Yarmouth
207-829-3269
Summer day camps open to ages 6-16.

★Chrysalis Acres
399 Pownal Road, Freeport
207-856-0047
www.chrysalisacres.com
Summer day camps open to ages 6 and up.

★Epona Farm
8 Faith Drive, Freeport
207-865-1808
Summer day camps for ages 8 and up with at least 6 months
of prior riding lesson experience.

★Perkins Farm
159 County Road, Gorham
207-839-2481
Lessons, dressage, jumping and hunt seat are offered.
Indoor and outdoor arenas, miles of trails. Summer camp for
children.

★Kent's Stables
726 Fort Hill Road, Gorham
207-839-6428
www.kentsstables.com

Outdoor stadium and a heated indoor arena. Miles of trail riding. Lessons for beginner to advanced. Summer camps.

HOT AIR BALLOONING

★Balloon Rides
291 State Street, Portland
727-510-9609   or   207-761-8373
www.hotairballoon.com
This is coastal Maine's oldest balloon rental ride company.
Breathtaking views await you as you float along above Casco Bay islands and the White Mountains.

Most flights begin near sunrise or just before sunset when the wind is lightest. Flight time is about one hour. Of course, all flights are subject to weather and pilot discretion, and ballooning involves a certain amount of risk. Their season runs from July 17 to September 15.

Reservations and deposit are required.

Other hot air balloon companies:

★Balloons Over New England
Toll Free: 800-788-5562

★Hot Fun-First Class Balloon Flights
2 Pine Road, Cape Elizabeth
207-799-0193

PAINTBALLING

Yes, parents of a certain age, paintballing is now considered a sport. What is paintball, you say? It is a game much like hide-n-seek where players try to find each other on a field and then 'tag' their opponents with a paintable 'marker' that resembles an odd-looking gun.

★Bennett Allweather Paintball
462 Fort Hill Road, Gorham
207-839-9177

★Firestorm Paintball
9 Storm Drive, Windham
127 North Road, Limington
General Info: 207-637-2940   Toll Free: 866-315-7044
www.firestormpaintball.com
Stadium lighting for night play, extreme fields, full-service pro shop, and airsmithing.

★Rogue Paintball
190 Northeast Road, Standish
www.RoguePaintball.com
207-642-7648

SKATEBOARDING

When MaineToday.com compiled their annual "Best" list, for the category "Best Skateboarding in Maine", Marginal Way in Portland was the top vote getter, with Windham Skate Park coming in second, and The Park in Bath pulling up third place.

★Brunswick Skate Park
McKeen Street. (Just before the high school)
Free street course.

★Dorcherd Zoo
Turn Point Road, Old Orchard Beach
Free street course with a vert ramp, open 24 hours a day.

★Freeport High School Skate Park
Mini ramp and a street course.

★Marginal Way, Portland
The city's only park built for skateboarding.

★The Park
26 Summer Street, Bath
207-443-8900
www.bathskatepark.com
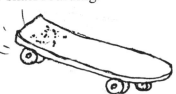
Maine's largest indoor skate park. Six foot half pipe with 7-foot extension connected to a hipped bowl with a double coping spine. Five-foot bank ramp, four-foot quarter pipe, tons of rails, 5 fun boxes.

★Rye Airfield
170 Lafayette Toad, Rye, New Hampshire
603-964-2800
www.ryeairfield.com
Open year-round, closed on Mondays
Rye Airfield is one of the largest, most advanced Extreme Sports Parks in the country. It is a year-round, modern facility located on 57 acres with lots of free parking.

This non-profit organization offers a state of the art 50,000 square foot indoor park, called Hanger One.

The facilities are geared towards all abilities and age groups in skateboarding, inline skating, and BMX riding.

Ramps, rails, minis, spines, bowls and pools abound. There is a 64-foot wide vert ramp that is 13 feet tall with 15-foot extensions and a 17-foot roll in.

Sessions last for 2 hours and 45 minutes.

★SPC Skatepark
Kennebunk
Indoor skatepark with a progressive, unique design - it is one huge mini ramp. This park is also the factory showroom for Skateparks, who have constructed parks all over New England.

★Windham Skate Park
Route 202, Windham (next to the Public Safety Building).
207-892-0547 or www.windhampolice.com/skatepark.htm
This supervised park has a half pipe, quarter pipes, bank ramps, pyramid, fun boxes, rails and concessions. Skateboards and rollerblades allowed but no bikes. For park hours check their website.

★ The Zone
33 Allen Avenue, Portland
207-878-SK89
Indoor park with a mini ramp, pro shop and a street course.

SKATING

When MaineToday.com asked readers in their annual poll to vote for their favorite ice skating spots, Deering Oaks took top honors, Mill Creek Park came in second and Falmouth Family Ice Arena pulled up third. We find that while Deering Oaks is lovely, Mill Creek Park is usually better maintained.

★Biddeford Ice Arena
Pomerleau Street, Alfred Road Business Park, Biddeford
207-283-0615
www.biddefordarena.com
The indoor arena offers an expanded schedule during school vacations as well as sessions and classes. Open to the public daily.

★Brunswick Town Common
Open for public skating from 9 a.m. to 10 p.m. daily.

★Colisee
190 Birch Street, Lewiston
207-783-2009
www.thecolisee.com
Lewiston-Auburn's Civic Center opens it indoor arena to the public from October to February. Call for days and times.

★Deering Oaks
State Street and Park Avenue, Portland
207-874-8793
Free outdoor pond.

★Falmouth Family Ice Arena
20 Hat Trick Drive, Falmouth
207-781-4200
www.familyice.org
This is a great spot located just off Route 1. It is an indoor skating facility that also includes an outdoor, refrigerated skating pond.

The Pond House is a modern but rustic looking warming hut with a massive stone chimney for both inside and outside fireplaces. The center has several learn-to-skate classes and sponsors several competitions.

★Freeport Middle School
Kendall Lane, Freeport
207-865-6171

★Mill Creek Park
Ocean Street at Hinckley, South Portland
207-767-7651
Free outdoor pond.

★Portland Ice Arena
225 Park Street, Portland
207-774-8553
Skate rentals and lessons, open for public skating.

★Roy Travis Arena at North Yarmouth Academy
495 U.S.Route 1, Yarmouth
207-846-2384

★Scarborough Wentworth Intermediate School
40 Gorham Road, Scarborough

★Westbrook Skating Rink
234 Pool Street, Biddeford
207-284-9652

★Yarmouth Community Services Park
Main Street, Yarmouth
Lighted rink with a warming hut.

SNOW SPORTS

See also Seacoast Fun Park, and Pinelands.

Whole books and countless articles have been devoted to Maine's magnificent ski areas. For a comprehensive listing call the SKI Maine Association (207-761-3774) or visit them online at www.skimaine.com.

If you are planning to head up to the mountains, you can check on the current ski conditions by calling (207-773-SNOW). We list here some of the more popular areas that can be considered a day trip from Portland.

There are some spots right in Greater Portland that are perfect for cross-country skiers. Try out: **Twin Brook**

Recreation Area off Tuttle Road in Cumberland; **Mast Landing Sanctuary** in Freeport; **Gilsland Farm** in Falmouth; **Smiling Hill Farm** in Westbrook; **Purpoddock Club** in Cape Elizabeth and the back side of **Evergreen Cemetery** behind the Westbrook College campus on Brighton Avenue. Also, call **Portland Trails** (207-775-2411) and request their excellent map of city trails where you can ski.

★Black Mountain of Maine
Rumford
207-364-8977
Located 75 miles from Portland, Black Mountain has a 470-foot vertical drop and 9 trails. They have 65% snowmaking capacity.

Double and triple chair lifts have recently been added to the existing T-bar and handle-tow. They offer night skiing, cross-country skiing, snow tubing, a ski school, equipment rental and a snack bar.

★Camden Snow Bowl Ski Area
Hosmer's Pond Road, Camden
207-236-3438 or SNO Phone 207-236-4418
www.camdensnowbowl.com
You will need to drive 85 miles (2 hours) to ski "Where the Mountains Meet the Sea", but you'll be met by a uniquely scenic snow bowl. Three lifts take you to eleven trails. They have night skiing, ski school, rentals, half-day tickets, a cafeteria and ice skating. You can fly downhill on the 400-foot toboggan chute where the U.S. National Tobogganing Championships are held each year.

With 950-feet of vertical drop and a 600-foot snow tubing park the place has a very family-friendly feel about it. They have one double chair lift, and for those of you who don't like to dangle from chair lifts, two T-bars take you to two easy trails.

★Clifford Park
Pool Street, Biddeford
The Clifford Park trail system is southern Maine's first municipal cross-country ski area with 2 ½ miles of trails. Beginning at the park entrance on Pool Street, it glides past the Westbrook skating rink before looping back to the park. While the 29-acre park offers ten routes, the main loop - Black Trail -swings past the granite landmark, 'Sliding Rock'.

★Lost Valley
Auburn
207-784-1561
www.lostvalleyski.com
You can ski all day, half day, at night - even hourly on Lost Valley's 15 trails. There is snowmaking and a snowboard terrain park. Lessons as well as rentals are available for alpine, cross-country and snowboarding.

There are 15 trails (six of them easy), two chairs, a T-bar and a half pipe.

If you would rather watch then ski, you can sit by the huge fieldstone fireplace in the glass-walled base lodge.

Lost Valley is about one hour north of Portland.

★Mt. Abram

240 Howe Hill Road, Greenwood

207-875-5002

www.skimtabram.com

Mt Abram is our favorite for family skiing. They offer 5 lifts, 39 trails and glades, a ski school, ski shop with rental, half-day tickets, child care, a cafeteria and two base lodges with a free shuttle service in between.

We love their beginner's Westside area and their ungroomed expert glade runs and race course, and the 1,325-foot Tubing Park.

They have chairlifts and for those of us who don't care to hang off chairlifts, Mt. Abram has 2 T-bars and one mini T-bar.

And if you have hot doggers who want the thrill of Sunday River, Mt. Abram is only about 20 minutes from Bethel. No wonder *Ski Magazine* has dubbed Mt. Abram, "A Little Gem".

★Pratt's Brook Park

Yarmouth

This 400-acre park provides cross-country ski trails for all levels. (See page 118)

★Shawnee Peak

Rte. 302, Bridgton

207-647-8444

www.shawneepeak.com

When there is little snow elsewhere in southern Maine, you can count on Shawnee with 98% snowmaking capacity. Formerly named Pleasant Mountain, it has a vertical drop of

1,300 feet and yet is less that one hour from Portland.

If you're having too good a time to leave, you might want to stay on for Shawnee's night skiing when 90% of the trails are open.

Two base lodges offer cafeterias, a nursery, ski school, ski shop/rental, a lounge and restaurant. One of the first slopes to welcome snowboarders, they have a White Water Snowboard Park.

Located 45 miles from Portland, Shawnee Park is also only 15 minutes from North Conway, New Hampshire with its sprawling shopping outlets.

★Sunday River
Bethel
Info: 207-824-3000 Snow Report: 207-824-6400
www.sundayriver.com
This is a huge resort that covers eight mountain peaks. Kids who like snowboarding will be impressed with the Upper Starlight, a snowboard-only park with a half pipe.

There are more than 100 ski trails with cutting edge snow making capacity top to bottom. Three base lodges, one summit lodge, day care, rentals, twelve lifts, sleigh rides and ice skating make Sunday River a big success.

Check out the Mountain Bike Park for May through October activity.

Located 67 miles north of Portland, it is about an hour and a half drive from the city.

SURFING

While there has always been a die hard core of Maine surfers, the sport has been steadily gaining in popularity with the younger set. Catching a wave in Maine is not always easy with the biggest waves occurring in fall and winter. Some people think that our ocean water is cold enough in July and August, thank you very much!

The following beaches are the most popular among surfers but some, like Higgins Beach, only allow surfing early in the morning and after 4:00 p.m. Try to hang ten at Ogunquit, Old Orchard, Wells, Higgins in Scarborough, Kennebunk and Popham Beach in Phippsburg. Long Sands/Short Sands in York, Gooch's Beach in Kennebunk and Scarborough Beach State Park are also local favorites.

There are two surf shops in Portland:

Moose County	Sunny Breeze Boardsports
610 Congress Street	425 Marginal Way
207-761-8084	207-775-2194

Excursions

See also L.L. Bean Outdoor Discovery Schools

■ADVENTURE BOUND RAFTING
Route 201, Caratunk
207-672-4300
www.adv-bound.com

This Youth and Family Outdoor Adventure Vacation Resort will custom tailor a one-day or multi-day package for you. They offer whitewater rafting, rock climbing, inflatable kayaking and ropes courses.

After your adventure, relax in their heated pool or 24-person hot tub. Caratunk is approximately a 2 ½ hour drive northwest from Portland.

■BURNT ISLAND LIGHTHOUSE
Boothbay Harbor
207-633-9580
www.maine.gov/dmr
Open late June through Labor Day, Monday through Friday
Admission includes water taxi ride: Adults $20; children $12
Board at Pier 8, departure times 12:15 p.m and 2:15 p.m.

Step off the boat and it is 1950. Harry Truman is president. This living history museum is brought to life with costumed interpreters who portray the original lighthouse keeper Joseph Muise, his wife Annie and children Adele, Prudence, Ann and Willard. Each one explains how their lives unfold and their roles in this real lighthouse keeper's family. Visitors arrive twice daily via the short boat ride to the island and are free to roam around and explore during their two-hour stay.

■CAMP WYONEGONIC FAMILY CAMP
215 Wyonegonic Road, Denmark
207-452-2051
www.wyonegonic.com
Cost: A typical 3-day session would be around $200 per individual, but prices vary depending on age and session.

How about going to summer camp *with* the kids for a change? In operation for nearly 100 years, Wyonegonic is the oldest girls camp in the United States. They seem to have caught onto something with their popular two, three, and five-day Family Camp sessions in August. Located on two and a half miles of private forested shoreline, families stay in rustic cabins with restrooms and shower houses located nearby.

Play tennis, wile away an afternoon in the craft shop or library. Enjoy swimming or sailing. Water-skiing, fishing, archery and horseback riding are also available.

Meals are provided in the main lodge/dining hall. Denmark is located on Route 117, about 45 miles (one hour) northwest of Portland. Wyonegonic has clay tennis courts, a variety of boats and miles of hiking and jogging trails on 300 acres of pine woods.

■CHILDREN'S MUSEUM OF PORTSMOUTH

280 Marcy Street, Portsmouth, New Hampshire
603-436-3853
www.childrens-museum.org
Open Tuesday through Saturday, 10 a.m. to 5 p.m.;
Sunday, 1 p.m. to 5 p.m. Open Mondays in the summer and
during school vacations.
Admission: Adults and children $6; senior citizens $5; under
age 1 free

Would your children like to know how their bones work, take
the controls on an exploration submarine or to see what a
butterfly looks like at 40 times its size?

These are only a few of the hands-on interactive
exhibits, daily activities, special workshops and performances
that make this museum a delightful place to visit.

Combine a day trip to the museum with a visit to
Strawbery Banke, Portsmouth's living museum, or a ferry ride
to the historic Isles of Shoales.

The museum is air-conditioned, has parking and a
shop that carries a good variety of books, puzzles, jewelry,
kits and more.

If You're in Portsmouth, Check Out:

Treehouse Toys
143 Market Street
and
G Willikers Toy Shop
13 Market Street or Fox Run Mall

■THE DOWNEASTER

100 Thompsons's Point Road, Portland
800-639-3317
www.thedowneaster.com
Trains run 365 days a year. Parking available $2 per day
Fares are $22 one way; $36 same day round-trip
Kids ages 2-15 ride half-fare every day and free on Sunday
From I-295 N, take exit 5 or from I-295 S, take exit 5A

Operated by Amtrak, the Downeaster provides four round-trips daily between Portland and Boston's North Station with eight stops in between. They share a space with Concord Trailways in the Portland Transportation Center. This makes it so easy to visit Boston for the day that over a million people have taken advantage of the comfortable ride and no parking hassles once in Boston. The possibilities are endless. North Station is under the same roof as Boston's Garden where the Bruins and Celtics teams play. It is also the site of many world-class concerts. Visit www.tdbanknorthgarden.com for a current events schedule.

You can walk to Fanieul Hall, the Aquarium, and the Freedom Trail from the station. Or grab a cab or subway train to the Children's Museum, Museum of Fine Arts, Science Museum, Public Garden swan boats, Fenway Park or the Frog Pond (rent skates in the winter).

Portland's train station is clean and modern. The train's amenities include comfortable seating with plenty of leg room, fold-down trays, electrical outlets (you can use your laptop and cell phone), and overhead reading lights. The Café Car serves drinks, light meals and snacks.

This is an all around winner for Portland families.

TIPS FOR THE DOWNEASTER

1. Make reservations early.
2. Bring photo identification.
3. The train car nearest the café often has a line of people in the aisle waiting to get in.
4. Keep to your seats when you stop to pick up new passengers as they may not know your seats are taken and there are no assigned seats.

■FALL FOLIAGE TOURING
www.visitmaine.com

Many Mainers will tell you that this is their favorite season with its warm days, cool nights and heart-stoppingly beautiful foliage.

And yes, we take our leaf peeping so seriously up here that there is actually a toll-free Foliage Hot Line (888-MAINE-45). The message is updated every couple of days through the end of October. Also, a web site hot line at www.maine.gov/doc/foliage.

But children are unlikely to be held rapt for hours on long drives along foliage trails. So here are some ideas that will take you into the heart of this vibrant season and let the children be equally entertained. Check the *Special Events* chapter and the internet address listed above for more ideas.

★Apple Saturday: Sabbathday Lake Shaker Museum, New Gloucester (Late September through mid-October) 207-926-4597

★Fryeburg Fair: Fryeburg (Late September to early October) This is Maine's oldest and largest agricultural fair.

★Cumberland Fair: Cumberland County Fairgrounds (Late September) www.cumberlandfair.com

★Common Ground Country Fair: Unity (Always the 3rd weekend after Labor Day) 207-568-4142

■GRAFTON NOTCH STATE PARK
Rt. 26, Bear River Road, Newry
In-season: 207-824-2912
Off-season: 207-624-6080
Open mid-May through mid-October
Fee charged

Located approximately a two-hour drive from Portland, Grafton Notch will reward you with breathtaking views of the White Mountains. The Appalachian Trail passes through this lovely area, resplendent with waterfalls, hiking trails, and picnic and fishing spots. Old Speck Mountain, Baldpate Mountain and Table Rock are three of the most prominent sites, but with the help of the park services map you won't want to miss the natural wonders of Screw Auger Falls, Mother Walker Falls and Moose Cave Gorge. There are also private campgrounds in the area.

Located off Route 26 between Upton and Newry, the park is about 75 miles northwest of Portland.

■INSIDE OUT PLAYGROUND
The Center, 93 Main Street, Waterville
207-877-8747
www.insideoutplayground.org
Open year-round, Monday - Thursday, 9 a.m. to 5 p.m;
Friday and Saturday, 9 a.m. to 7 p.m.; closed Sundays
Admission: $5 per child a day; $4 per child an hour; under
age 1 free; $12 household maximum

This non-profit organization features 6,000-square feet of
space where children can explore a two-story castle,
playhouse, pirate ship, hundreds of toys, a room full of
blocks and several riding toys. It is Maine's only indoor
playground.
Waterville is 78 miles from Portland.

■ISLES OF SHOALS STEAMSHIP CO.
315 Market Street, Portsmouth, New Hampshire
800-441-4621 or 603-431-5500
www.islesofshoals.com
Open: Ferries service the Isles from mid-June to Labor Day
(rain or shine).
Cost: Adults $24; children (ages3-12) $14; senior (60+) $19;
military $19

In 1614, Virginia's Captain John Smith first landed on these
nine granite-bound islands. The following centuries brought
pirates, cod fishermen and finally, tourists and small hotels
catering to the likes of Nathaniel Hawthorne, Mark Twain and
the renowned Maine author Sarah Orne Jewett.

This is where the poet Celia Thaxter (1835-1894) wrote her well-known book, *An Island Garden.*

The Steamship company offers a narrated Isles of Shoals and Portsmouth Harbor Tour where you'll view the nine islands, three lighthouses, five forts, and the naval yard and prison. The Star Island Stopover tour is one of their most popular. It lasts three hours and you'll experience the island atmosphere of our colonial ancestors and hear stories of ghosts, pirates and buried treasure!

■KELMSCOTT FARM
12 Van Cycle Road, Lincolnville
207-763-4088
www.kelmscott.org
Open: May 1 - October 31, 10 a.m. to 5 p.m.;
November 1 - April 30, 10 a.m. - 3 p.m.; closed Mondays
Admission: Adults $5; children 4-15 $3; under 4 free

Over one hundred Cotswald sheep covered with curly dread locks greet you at this rare breeds foundation located on 147 acres. The non-profit conservation and education center is home to some animals that are literally the last of their kind. Over 200 breeds of rare livestock live here, among them are llamas and Gloucestershire Old Spots pigs. Activities such as wagon rides, story times and felting fun are offered. Self-guided tours are always available when the farm is open. The Wool Shed Museum and Gift Shop sell many items.

Lincolnville is approximately 100 miles northeast of Portland. It is located in the mid-coast area near Camden, Belfast and Castine.

■KENNE*BEAR*PORT ANNUAL TEDDY BEAR SHOW
Kennebunkport
207-967-0857
www.visitthekennebunks.com or
www.maine.info/festivals11.html
Admission: Adults $5; children and seniors $2; children under 5 free

This event is usually held the first or second weekend in August at a local school. Sponsored by the Kennebunk, Kennebunkport Chamber of Commerce, it features over 40 exhibitors and bear artists from across the nation selling teddy bears and teddy bear related items. Free drawings throughout the day.

■LOBSTER BOAT RACING
www.lobsterboatracing.com
When: June through August; all races begin at 10:00 a.m.

Nothing is more Maine than a day at the lobster boat races! These events have grown into a summer tradition in local harbors and most of the boats are actual working lobster boats.

In 2006, seven locations presented sanctioned events. A seventh race in Pemaquid draws lots of boats and spectators for a "just for fun" afternoon of racing.

★Boothbay Harbor (about an hour north of Portland) offers some of the best views for land-bound spectators. The lead off race is between Tumbler and McFarland Islands inside the harbor. Get a viewing spot on Atlantic Avenue

along the harbor's east shore. Race day is in June (207-633-4900).
    ★Harpswell's race course has been located in Potts Harbor. Race day is usually in July (207-833-6147).
    ★Pemaquid's race is held in August (207-563-8707).

■MAINE DISCOVERY MUSEUM
74 Main Street, Bangor
207-262-7200
www.mainediscoverymuseum.org
Open: Tuesday - Saturday, 9:30 a.m. to 5:00 p.m.; Sunday, noon to 5:00 p.m. Closed Mondays except some school holidays.
Admission: Adults and children $6.00; children under 1 free

Conveniently located off I-95, this is the largest interactive children's museum north of Boston with three floors of hands-on activities and exhibits.
    Kids send boats down the 20-foot river in Nature Trails and explore the globe in Passport while learning to navigate the world in a Mapmobile.
    Travel through Maine's best-loved children's literary classics in Booktown. Kids sculpt, press their bodies on a giant pin screen and make a picture using colored light rods in the Artscape area.
    A big hit with kids is to videotape themselves singing in the sound studio. *Too Much Fun*! is the gift shop featuring educational toys and children's books.
    Parking is available in the Pickering Square Parking Garage located behind the museum.

■MAINE WILDERNESS TOURS
7 Croquet Lane, Belgrade
207-465-4333
www.mainewildernesstours.com

Fishing, kayaking, canoeing, hiking, snowmobiling and moose watching trips offered for ½ day up to week-long excursions.
 With over 125 different outdoor related trips they have something for almost everyone.

■MEAD MILL TOURS
15 Hartford Street, Rumford
207-369-2589
Call to reserve your tour for July or August.
Admission: free

Learn how paper is made, discover the Rumford Mill and see paper makers at work. Half-day forest tours plus full Mill tours are offered as well as all-day forest tours.
 Kids World of Fun and Wonder is also located in Rumford. Rumford is located approximately 80 miles from Portland.

■MOUNT WASHINGTON COG RAILWAY
Route 302, Bretton Woods, New Hampshire
In NH: 603-278-5404 Toll Free: 800-922-8825
www.thecog.com
Open year-round for skiers, riders and sightseers

Just 2 ½ hours from Portland you can enjoy a three-mile ride to the summit of Mount Washington on the world's first mountain-climbing railway. Built in 1869, the tracks climb up the White Mountains and on a clear day, the view from the summit spans four states, limited only by the curvature of the earth.

At the base, you can visit their museum, eat lunch at the cafeteria or visit the gift shop.

Once at the Summit, visit the mile-high state park including The Sherman Adams Observation Center.

Advance ticket purchase by phone or at the Base Station is recommended.

■OWL'S HEAD TRANSPORTATION MUSEUM
Rt. 73, Owl's Head
207-594-4418
www.owlshead.org
Open: Daily year-round; Nov.- March, 10 a.m to 4 p.m.;
April - October, 10 a.m. to 5 p.m.
Admission: Adults $7; children $5; under 5 free; family maximum $18

Three miles south of Rockland, this museum maintains one of the finest and most extensive collections of various modes of transportation.

Pioneer era aircraft and historically significant automobiles, carriages, bicycles, motorcycles and engines are maintained in operating condition. The museum holds many special events featuring actual demonstrations of their collections. Spectacular air shows accompany most events.

Call or send for their events schedule. With educational tours and programs and a museum gallery and store, restoration facility, 60-acre nature park, children's park and picnic area you will find this a full trip.

Owl's Head is 85 miles north of Portland.

■PERHAM'S OF WEST PARIS

Rt. 26 and 219, 194 Bethel Road, West Paris
207-674-2341 or 800-371-GEMS
Open: Year-round, daily 9 a.m. to 5 p.m.
Admission free

Perham's is located about an hour and 15 minutes north of Portland, but we think it is worth the ride. If you are skiing at either Mt. Abrams or Sunday River, Perham's is on the way.

This is a large jewel, gem and mineral store located in an area that is noted for its deposits of tourmaline, feldspar, mica and quartz. The shop, featured on the Discovery Channel, was founded in 1919 by Stan Perham, dubbed the "Gem Man at Trap Corner" in a *Reader's Digest* article. Today his family continues the business as it draws an international clientele of 100,000 every year.

After a visit to their Mineral Museum (free), exhibiting one of the finest existing collections of Maine minerals and gems, rockhounds of all ages will be ready to visit one of the store's five quarries which are open free of charge. Perham's will provide you with quarry maps upon request and you may keep the specimens you find in the nearby Oxford Hills.

In October 1972, two men searching an abandoned

mining site in western Maine found over two million carats of gem tourmaline, a quantity so large that jewelers are still cutting gems today.

  The store sells professional picks, or you can bring your own. Also, remember the bug spray as the mosquitoes can be thick up this way.

■POLAND SPRING PRESERVATION PARK
115 Preservation Way, Poland Spring
207-998-7143
www.polandspring.com
Open: Year-round, 8 a.m. to 4 p.m.; closed Mondays.

Bottled and sold throughout the world, Poland Spring Natural Spring Water is America's top brand of bottled water.

  The white marble Spring House, now part of this park, looks out through a window at the original spring, called simply "The Source". Developed by Poland Spring Bottling Co. this is a lovely place with a pond and beautiful grounds. There is a museum, visitor center, Sadie's Place Café, gift shop, a Maine artists gallery and interactive earth science and product displays as well as a virtual tour of today's Poland Spring bottling plant.

  Trail maps are available in the gift shop for $1 and they detail seven trails on the property that offer about 4 miles of hiking. The trails are clearly marked with the longest about 1.2 miles.

  The park is located on Route 26 in Poland Spring, 10 miles north of Gray and 40 miles from Portland.

■*THE POLAR EXPRESS*

North Conway Depot, North Conway, New Hampshire and
Hobo Railroad, Lincoln, New Hampshire
603-447-3100
www.polarexpress.org
Open between Thanksgiving and Christmas
Admission varies depending on seating, but is around $35
Wheelchair accessible

Climb the train tracks by moonlight as children and parents
reenact Chris Van Allsburg's now classic book, *The Polar
Express.* The proceeds of this magical journey to the North
Pole benefit literacy programs.

Stay warm and cozy drinking the hot chocolate served
by chefs in tall white hats, until the train arrives at a lodge and
Van Allsburg's adventure continues.

All believers ride back down with reindeer bells in
their pockets. Plan on about two hours.

Due to the incredible popularity of this event, tickets
are available through a mail-in lottery system ONLY. The
deadline has been September 30 in the past.

Names are randomly drawn from all entries in mid-
October and tickets will be sold as the winners are contacted
that same day. People from as far away as Texas come to ride
the trains!

A second train ride has been added and run by the
Hobo Railroad in Lincoln, New Hampshire.

■PUFFIN CRUISES
Maine Audubon Society, Boothbay Harbor
207-781-2330
http://projectpuffin.org/tour.html
Cruises run in the summer months

Six miles off Pemaquid Point lies Eastern Egg Rock, home to the Audubon Society's successful puffin-restoration efforts.

June and July are the best months for taking one of these naturalist-guided boat tours with an Audubon or other local captain.

Before you go, buy or borrow from the library the book *Project Puffin: How We Brought Puffins Back to Egg Rock* by Stephen W. Kress as told to Pete Salmansohn. It is a great story about what one person can do to make a difference.

■PORT OF PORTSMOUTH MARITIME MUSEUM AND ALBACORE PARK
600 Market Street, Portsmouth, New Hampshire
603-436-3680
www.portsmouthnh.com/thingstodo/index.cfm
Open: USS Albacore, May 1 through Columbus Day, 9:30 a.m. to 5:30 p.m. Call for winter hours.
Admission: Adults $5; children 7-17 $3; military $4; under 7 free

Year-round guided tours explore a U.S. Navy submarine and see first-hand how a crew of 55 men worked and lived aboard a 205' by 27' sub. Located in Albacore Park, it is a memorial to all those who served in the submarine service. Located across the street from The Port of Portsmouth Maritime Museum, the park includes a visitor's center, a small museum and a gift shop.

Portsmouth is a one-hour drive south of Portland unless there is a lot of traffic.

■SANTA'S VILLAGE
Rt. 2, Jefferson, New Hampshire
603-586-4445
www.santasvillage.com
Open: Late May until mid-June, Saturday and Sunday only; mid-June to early September, daily; early September through December, Saturday and Sunday only. Call ahead for times. Admission: $21.50; ages 62+ $19.50; ages 1-3 are Santa's Guest with a paid adult. One price includes admission and unlimited rides and performances.

Celebrating over 50 years of talking reindeer and snowmen as tall as trees, all children should make this trek once. During the summer months when the village is open daily, you can ride a Reindeer Coaster and splash down the Yule Log Flume. There are 16 action-packed rides and a variety of live performances. Children can create crafts in Santa's Workshop, decorate their own gingerbread man, and play the "Elfabet Game" for prizes.

Visit their web site for a taste of what is in store. This being the 21st century, you can even email Santa from this site.

■SEACOAST SCIENCE CENTER
570 Ocean Blvd., Odiorne State Park, Rye, New Hampshire
603-436-8043
www.seacentr.org
Open: Year-round. April-October, daily
November-March, Saturday through Monday
Center admission: Adults $3; ages 3-12 $1
Park entrance: Adults $3; ages 6-11 $1

Located in lovely Odiorne State Park, the Seacoast Science Center is situated on 136 acres. Offering a rich combination of educational programs, entertainment and exhibits, there are programs for families throughout the year including tide pool tours, early morning bird walks and more. Since the Center opened in 1992, over 1 million people have visited.

The Center has several aquariums and hands-on marine exhibits, including a 1,000-gallon Gulf of Maine tank. The Nature Store offers a nice selection of books and gifts.

Odiorne State Park is a great place to go tide pooling and wading after your museum visit. Use one of the grills and picnic tables and enjoy this scenic spot.

■SONGO RIVER QUEEN II
Route 302, (on the Causeway) Naples
www.songoriverqueen.net
207-693-6861
Open June through September, daily
Cost varies by length and trip

Sebago Lake is Maine's second largest lake, attracting thousands of visitors and campers to its peaceful shores. A wonderful way to tour the outlying lakes and the old canal system between Sebago and Long Lake is a cruise on the faux-steamship Songo Queen.

This is a charming replica of a Mississippi River stern wheeler, with a small snack bar and restroom facilities on board. They offer a variety of cruises including an end of the day trip to watch the sun set over the mountains.

But the Songo River Queen is only one of the fun things to do on the Causeway. You can rent pedal-boats, bumper boats, inner tubes that are like bumper cars on water, jet-skis or take a parasail ride. An arcade, mini-golf course, restaurants, candy and ice cream shops are all located within easy walking distance of each other.

■STORYLAND
Route 16, Glen, New Hampshire
www.storylandnh.com
603-383-4186
Open weekends only Memorial Day to Father's Day.
After Father's Day to Labor Day, open daily
Labor Day to Columbus Day, weekends only
Admission: $22 per person; age 3 and under free
Pay-one-price admission is good for a full day of adventure and includes unlimited rides, shows and many activities.

This children's theme park is geared for the young family with spotlessly maintained grounds and gardens. Consider it pre-Disney preparation.

They do a great job of being family friendly with diapers sold at all their gift shops, Mama's Houses adjacent to restrooms for nursing mothers and free strollers.

Picnic lunches are welcome or treat the family at the Flying Carpet Sandwich Oasis or the Whistle Stop Ice Cream and Fried Dough stand.

Attractions include Whirling Whales, Swan Boats, Antique Cars, Farm Follies, a Sandcastle Maze, StoryLand Queen, Cinderella's Castle, and Dr. Geyser's Remarkable Raft Ride, to name just a few.

■STRAWBERY BANKE MUSEUM
Marcy and Hancock Streets, Portsmouth, New Hampshire
Info: 603-433-1100   Museum Shop: 603-433-1114
www.strawberybanke.org
Open: May 1 through October 31, daily;
November 1 to April 30, Thursday - Sunday
Special holiday events at Thanksgiving and Christmas.
Closed January and holidays.

Founded in 1630, this historic waterfront neighborhood got its name (yes, it is spelled with one "r") from the wild berries that grew on the banks of the Piscataqua River.

The lovingly restored site consists of 10 furnished houses and period gardens representing different periods in American history. Costumed interpreters portray residents and merchants. Your family can watch potters, a blacksmith and a boat builder at work in several exhibit houses. A variety of educational and fun activities are offered for children.

The Candlelight Stroll in December would be a lovely, historical and non-commercial way to celebrate the season with children.

Think of combining this trip with a visit to the Portsmouth Children's Museum located just two blocks away.

■WINDJAMMING
800-807-WIND
www.sailmainecoast.com
Sail season is mid-May to mid-October

The Maine Windjammer Association can put you in touch with several different Windjammer tours. There is no better way to explore Maine's rugged coast than on a day sail or a 3, 4, or 6-day cruise. Delicious food and expert crews leave from Camden, Rockland and Rockport. Prices range from $395 to $875 and include meals.

Sunday evenings from June through September go down to the Camden wharf and join the people who sit and watch the passengers board these white cloud vessels to cruise out into Penobscot Bay. Saturday afternoon, the week-long excursion over, the people head back down to watch the ships return. Camden is the windjammer capital of the world.

Downeast Windjammer Cruises in Bar Harbor (www.downeastwindjammer.com) is another outfit that offers daily morning, afternoon and sunset cruises (207-288-4585).

Also, Schooner Olad (www.maineschooners.com) provides 2-hour sails that depart from Camden Harbor (207-236-2323).

Room for Notes

Shopping.....briefly

THE OLD PORT EXCHANGE, PORTLAND

Certainly one of the finest urban renovation projects on the East Coast, the Old Port Exchange area crackles with creativity. Stylish restaurants, shops and galleries housed in refurbished historic buildings blend in with the downeast waterfront character.

The Old Port is home to many artists and craftspeople as well as some quality children's toy stores. Treehouse Toys (www.treehousetoys.com) at 47 Exchange Street is everything a huge impersonal chain store is not. Loaded with beautiful books and toys from the latest craze to the classics, you are charmed the minute you pass through the door. Take a break from shopping and treat yourself to a latte or cappuccino at JavaNet at 37 Exchange Street. You can check your emails while the kids have a hot chocolate.

Northern Sky Toyz located at 388 Fore Street sells an array of the latest and most creative kites as well as a variety of toys and books.

Bordered by Commercial, Congress, Union and Pearl Streets, the area overlooks a vibrant working waterfront where ferries and lobster boats make for a lively scene. Narrow cobbled streets were mostly built after a devastating fire in 1866.

There is a limited amount of on-street parking in the area. See *Parking in Portland* (page 6). Some more shops that you might want to visit are:

Apple Bee Co., 370 Fore Street (toys & books)
Beal's Famous Ice Cream, 12 Moulton Street
Books, Etc., 38 Exchange Street
Bull Moose Music, 151 Middle Street
Casablanca Comics & Games, 151 Middle Street
Casco Bay Books, 151 Middle Street
Communiques, 3 Moulton Street
Cotton Garden, 55 Exchange Street (clothing)
Old Port Candy Co., 422 Fore Street

For a list of stores in Portland's Downtown and Arts District as well as the Old Port Exchange, call The Downtown District (207-772-6828) or visit www.portlandmaine.com.

THE MAINE MALL

Located off the Maine Turnpike in South Portland, the Maine Mall is the largest super-mall in Maine with over 140 stores plus 18 restaurants, many located in the central Food Court.

Buffeted by Sears, Macy's, Best Buy, Sports Authority and J.C Penney, here are some of the stores of interest to parents:

Borders	Waldenbooks/WaldenKids
Build-A-Bear	Children's Place
Claires Etc.	Gap Kids/Baby Gap
Electronics Boutique	Gymboree
Disney Store	KB Toys
Lids	Motherhood Maternity

For a more complete list of stores in the Maine Mall call
(207-774-0303) or visit www.mainemall.com.

FREEPORT

Located seventeen miles north of Portland, Freeport is a 170-
store shopper's Mecca stretching for the most part along its
Main Street and immediate side streets. Anchored by the
extraordinarily successful L.L. Bean (yes, they are open 365
days a year), many stores and outlets offer children's goods.

There are many excellent guides to the Freeport
shopping area and once you are there, a simple map can be
obtained everywhere that lists the stores and their locations.
The following is a short list of some of the stores of interest
if you are shopping with or for kids.

Gap/Gap Kids	The Beadin Path
J. Crew Factory Store	Sherman's Bookstore
Soccer Mainea	A. Wilbur's Candy Shoppe
L.L. Bean	Cool As A Moose
Oshkosh B'Gosh	Patagonia Outlet
Carter's Childrenswear	Play and Learn
Ben & Jerry's Ice Cream	puzzles & games etc.
Mangy Moose	

For more information call the Freeport Merchants Association
(207-865-1212) or visit www.freeportusa.com.

KITTERY

Located just one hour south of Portland on Coastal Route 1, Kittery has over 130 factory outlets, offering 20% to 75% off on merchandise. As with the Freeport shopping area to the north of Portland, many of the stores here offer children's goods. Don't miss Kittery Trading Post with three floors of everything you need for the outdoors. Children especially enjoy the displays of animal wildlife found around the store, with a big hit being the large stuffed Maine moose. They carry children's casual clothing, outerwear and footwear, as well as educational books and games. Every fall they hold a special Septemberfest event starting on Labor Day with pony rides, animal tracking, clowns, spincasting, scouting skills and wildlife seminars.

We suggest a partial list of stores you might want to visit in Kittery:

Bass Shoe   hanna andersson
Big Dog Sportswear   Old Navy
Book Warehouse   Hartstrings Childrenswear
Carters Childrenswear   OshKosh B'Gosh
KB Toys   Skechers
Gap Outlet   Sweatshirt Shop
Stride-Rite/Keds

For a complete list of factory outlet stores, call the Kittery Outlet Association (888-548-8379) or visit them at www.thekitteryoutlets.com.

Special Events

T he Cumberland County Civic Center, One Civic Center Square, Portland, ME 04101 attracts major events and concerts throughout the year. They have hosted the Harlem Globetrotters, concerts, Sesame Street Live, Disney on Ice, and Nickelodeon. From October to May they are also home to the Portland Pirates, the AHL affiliate of the Mighty Ducks of Anaheim hockey team. Tickets to the Civic Center events are available at the Civic Center Ticket Office and all Ticketmaster locations. For more information visit www.theciviccenter.com or to order tickets by phone, call the Box Office (207-775-3458). There is also a 24-hour event information hot line (207-775-3825 ext.500). The box office is open Monday through Saturday, 9:30 a.m. to 5:30 p.m. and Sunday 10 a.m. to 4 p.m.

A good website for current scheduled events in the area is www.mainetourism.com also check the local listings. Remember dates and locations change, so always check before making plans.

JANUARY

Maine Winterfest. aka Maine Snow & Ice Follies.
Freeport and Falmouth. Family winter fun includes sledding, skating, ice carving competitions and demonstrations, live concerts and games. Contact: 207-772-2811 or www.mainewinterfest.com

FEBRUARY

U.S. National Toboggan Championships. Camden Snow Bowl. Watch as more than 250 teams from across the U.S. fly down the 400-foot run. Later, you can rent a sled and swosh down the specially built run yourself. Events take place all weekend.
Contact: 207-236-3438 or www.camdensnowbowl.com.

Musher's Bowl & Skijoring Race. Bridgton. Three fun-filled days of ice-fishing, polar bear dunk, snowmobile rides, fireworks, food and contests. Watch over 100 dog teams compete. Contact: 207-647-3472 or www.musherbowl.com.

Winter Carnival. Kennebunk. Variety show, magic, chili/chowder contest, children's games, ice skating and snow sculpture contest. Most events free. Contact: 207-967-0857 or www.kennebunkmaine.org.

Longfellow's Birthday Party. Portland. Maine Historical Society's family program honors poet Henry Wadsworth Longfellow's birthday every February 25th. Children are read some of his favorite poems, they write their own poems and eat birthday cake. Free.
Contact: 207-774-1822 or www.mainehistory.org.

MARCH

Family Nature Walk: Signs of Spring. Gilsland Farm, Falmouth. Audubon educator leads exploration of the sanctuary in search of signs of spring and wildlife. Contact: 207-781-2330 or www.maineaudubon.org.

Maine Maple Sunday. STATEWIDE! Maple sugar houses open their doors to the public. Held the fourth Sunday in March (see *Farms & Orchards)*. Contact: 207-287-3871 or www.getrealmaine.com.

The Portland Flower Show. Portland. Just when you think summer will never come it arrives in glorious gardens, a children's area, food court and plenty of landscaping displays. Contact:800-251-1784 or www.portlandcompany.com/flower.

APRIL

Spring Celebration & Calf Watch. Wolfe's Neck Farm, Freeport. Contact: 207-865-4469 or www.wolfesneck.org.

Eggs-Citing Egg-Splat Contest. Portland Observatory, Munjoy Hill, Portland. Carefully wrap your own egg and then drop it from the top of the 92-foot observatory. Best overall creative design that survives the fall and hits the target wins $25. Register early as there is a limit of 50 children. For 1st through 5th graders. Contact: 207-756-8275.

Earth Day Celebration. Gilsland Farm, Falmouth. Service-oriented projects at several of the sanctuaries. Contact: 207-761-2330 or www.maineaudubon.org.

Fisherman's Festival. Boothbay Harbor. Weekend celebration offers a slippery codfish relay race, a boat parade, kids activities, the Miss Shrimp Princess pageant and a blessing-of-the-fleet ceremony. Contact: 207-633-2353 or www.boothbayharbor.com.

Portland Sea Dogs. Portland. Season opens. All home games at Hadlock Field. Contact: 207-879-8500 or www.portlandseadogs.com.

MAY

Rockhound Roundup. Portland. Held at University of Maine. Maine's largest gem, rock, jewelry and mineral show. Contact: Maine Mineralogical Society. Check local listings for dates. Contact: 207-284-6206.

Maine State Parade. Lewiston. Celebrate spring with the largest parade in Maine. Colorful floats, clowns, high school bands. Contact 207-828-6666 or www.wcsh6.com.

Maine Mineral Symposium. Augusta. Sponsored by the Maine Geological Survey. Rock-related exhibits, dealers, lectures and field trips to local quarries. Contact: 207-287-7178.

Cinco de Mayo Celebration. Portland. The Center for Cultural Exchange celebrates with Mexican food and music in Longfellow Square. Contact: 207-761-1545 or www.centerforculturalexchange.org.

JUNE

LaKermesse. Biddeford. Weekend long Franco-American festival includes fireworks, a parade and tents filled with crafts, entertainment, and food. Contact: 207-283-1889 or www.lakermesse.org.

Old Port Festival. Portland. A morning parade from City Hall to the restored historic district of the city. Six stages of music, foods from around the world, stilt walkers, games, rides and puppets. Free admission. Contact: 207-772-6828 or www.portlandmaine.com.

Saco Sidewalk Art Festival. Main Street, Saco. One of the largest of the early summer festivals with over 150 exhibitors displaying watercolors, graphics, photographs, silkscreening and sculpture. Contact: 207-282-6169.

Paddle Sports Festival. Freeport. A weekend devoted to the kayaking and canoeing enthusiasts with lessons, lectures and paddling adventures. Pre-registration is required for lessons, but drop-ins are welcome for all other events. Sponsored by L.L. Bean. Contact: 800-559-0747 ext. 37222.

Greek Heritage Festival. Portland. Greek food, live Greek band, dance ensembles, videos, bookstore and numerous kid's activities. Contact: 207-774-0281 or www.greek-fest.com.

JULY

Bates Dance Festival. Lewiston. Various public events, many free. Features choreographers, dancers, educators and students from around the world.
Contact: 207-786-6381 or ww.bates.edu.

Fourth of July Celebrations. Various locations. The Portland Symphony Orchestra holds spectacular outdoor Pops concerts at various locales on and around the 4th. Concerts end with a fireworks display. In the past they have been held at Highland Green in Topsham, Fort Williams in Cape Elizabeth and Shawnee Peak in Bridgton.
Contact: 207-842-0800 or www.portlandsymphony.com

Native American Pow Wow. Harbor Park, Wells. Music, dance, crafts, jewelry demonstrations.
Contact: 207-646-2451.

Maine Festival. Brunswick. Conceived over 25 years ago to showcase Maine's native talent, the state's largest festival has been going strong for several years at Thomas Point Beach. Every kind of entertainment and display imaginable. Dancers, storytellers, clowns and over 500 artists and craftspeople. A separate children's area provides hands-on activities. Call first as the festival has been held at different locations in other years. Contact: 207-772-9012 or www.mainearts.com.

Bowdoin Summer Music Festival. Brunswick. A summer long, classical chamber music program with various concerts at Bowdoin College. Contact: 207-373-1443 or www.summermusic.org.

Maine Farm Day. Various locations. Many farms are open to the public. Contact: Dept. of Agriculture for a list. 207-287-3491.

Yarmouth Clam Festival. Yarmouth. Held in mid-July. Free horse-drawn wagon rides, face painting, pancake breakfast, balloon zoo, canoe race and contests for kids. Contact: 207-846-3984 or www.clamfestival.com.

AUGUST

Festival de Joie. Lewiston. Celebrate everything Franco from a café serving food as it was eaten 250 years ago in France to lots of entertainment, much of it in French. Contact: 207-782-6231 or www.festivaldejoie.org.

Sidewalk Arts Festival. Portland. This annual summertime tradition draws as many as 60,000 people. Hundreds of artists' booths line Congress Street. Contact: 207-828-6666 or www.wcsh6.com/community.

Spring Point Festival. South Portland. Pancake breakfast. Sand castle contest, many children's games, a dog show and crafts. Contact: 207-767-7602.

Art in the Park. Mill Creek Park, South Portland. Stroll around the open booths to admire paintings, photographs and all manner of art by artists from the entire eastern seaboard. Contact: 207-767-7605.

Mt. Agamenticus Jazz & Blues Festival. York. Great music, food, and a children's tent. Contact: 207-363-1040.

Great Falls Balloon Festival. Lewiston-Auburn. A 60-foot tall flying purple people-eater drifts in the sky next to a 70-foot Shamu along the shores of the Androscoggin River. Along with all the hot air balloons there are concerts, parades, kid's activities, and a photo contest. Contact: 207-782-2637 or www.greatfallsballoonfestival.org.

Festival of Cultural Exchange. Portland. Experience music, art, food and dance from all over the world. Tickets can be purchased in advance. Contact: 207-761-1545 or www.centerforculturalexchange.org.

Maine Highland Games. Brunswick. All things Scottish at Thomas Point Beach. Food, music, dance. Contact: 207-549-7451 or www.mainehighlandgames.org

Beach to Beacon 10K Road Race. Cape Elizabeth. Founded by Maine's Olympic gold-medalist Joan Benoit Samuelson, the event now draws over 4,000 athletes from around the world to run from Crescent Beach to Fort Williams. There is a children's 1K race. Contact: 888-480-6940 or www.Beach2Beacon.org/

Annual Beach Olympics. Old Orchard Beach. Beach games with Olympic atmosphere. Prizes, entertainment, food, and family fun. Contact: 207-934-2500 or www.oldorchardbeachmaine.com

Riverfest. Kennebunk. Bring your swimsuit for family canoe races, decorated duck races with a cash prize in the little duck race. Games, food and live entertainment. Contact: 207-969-0857.

SEPTEMBER

Civil War Re-enactment. Pettingill Farm, Freeport. Contact 207-865-3170.

Cumberland Fair. Cumberland Center. Largest Holstein Futurity in the country. International horse and ox pull, goat, rabbit and livestock shows, calf and pig scrambles, MacDonald's Children's Farm. Variety of 4-H displays. Contact: 207-829-5531.

Fall in the Village Art Festival. Freeport. The works of over 100 New England artists are displayed throughout the village. Contact: 207-865-1212.

The Common Ground Fair. Unity. Started over 25 years ago by the Maine Organic Farmers and Gardeners Association. Activities include live animal demonstrations, crafts, exhibition halls with wooden toys. Lots of children's activities. Contact: 207-568-4142.

Capriccio Festival of the Arts. Ogunquit. Kite flying festival on the beautiful Ogunquit Beach. Family activities and concerts. Contact: 207-646-6170 or www.ogunquit.org.

 **OCTOBER**

Ghost Train. Boothbay Harbor Railway Village. Contact: 207-633-4727 or www.railwayvillage.org.

Fryeburg Fair. Fryeburg. You can just follow the traffic to Maine's largest fair. Over 300,000 visitors come to see the livestock and taste the fresh-baked pies. Children love the goat judging and the llamas, pigs, cattle, and exotic poultry. There are rides, an exhibition hall, entertainment and games. Contact: 207-935-3268 or www.fryeburgfair.com

Farm Tours & Hayrides. Wolfe's Neck Farm, Freeport. Explore the farm and enjoy a scenic pumpkin hayride. Contact: 207-865-4363 or www.wolfesneckfarm.org

NOVEMBER

Five Weeks of Christmas. Bath. Special events through the holiday season that include a parade, sings, craft fairs, and several children's events. Contact: 207-442-7291 or www.visitbath.com.

Monument Square Tree Lighting Ceremony. Portland. Costumed carolers, Father Christmas, free wagon rides. Contact: 207-772-6828.

DECEMBER

Note: Tree lighting ceremonies are held in most towns.

Sparkle Weekend: Freeport. Hayrides, a parade of lights, horse-drawn carriages, carolers, a talking Christmas tree, picture taking with Santa at his castle and a 5K jingle bell run. Tubas playing songs of the season. Contact: 207-865-1212 or www.freeportusa.com/sparkle.

Longfellow Family Christmas. Portland. Hosted by the Maine Historical Society with house tours, a book fair and Victorian children's activities. Contact: 207-774-1822.

Christmas Prelude. Kennebunkport. A lobster boat heralds Santa's arrival in this charming village, revelers enjoy a variety of street entertainers, pancake breakfasts and crafts. Contact: 207-967-0857or www.christmasprelude.com.

Santafest & *The Polar Express.* Portland. Ride the Narrow Gauge Railroad for the three-mile trip to view over 200 holiday displays. Have cookies and cider and meet Santa. Contact: 207-828-0814 or www.mngrr.org/

Maine Writers and Publishers Alliance Holiday Book Signing and Sale. Brunswick. Features over 25 well-known authors and a children's reading. Admission is free at the Curtis Memorial Library and books are available for sale with authors on hand to sign. Contact: 207-725-1014 or www.mainewriters.org.

Family Festival: Lighting of the Copper Beech Tree. Portland. The annual lighting at the Portland Museum of Art. Take part in art-making, food, music, visits with Santa and a sing-along. Located on High Street. Free. Contact: 207-775-6148.

Coats & Toys for Kids Day. Statewide. Gently-used coats and toys are collected and distributed to kids in need. Call if your school or organization wants to take part. Contact: 207-774-6304.

Holiday Craft Fair & Children's Night Tree Program. Wolfe's Neck Farm, Freeport. After a reading of Eve Bunting's *Night Tree,* ornaments are made to hang in the forest. Space limited. Contact: 207-865-4363.

Colby College's Festival of Carols & Lights. Waterville. A musical prelude is followed by Advent and Christmas readings, caroling, a capella groups and concludes with the congregation singing *Silent Night.* Contact: 207-873-3315 or www.colby.edu/news_events.

Christmas at Victoria Mansion. Portland. Tour the dazzlingly decorated Mansion and shop for unique Victorian style cards, gifts, toys, jewelry and decoration.
Contact: 207-772-4841 or visit www.victoriamansion.org

New Year's Portland. Portland. December 31st. A spectacular event begun in 1984 and now attracting more than 10,000 people to 150 shows at over 25 locations. Mostly concentrated from Congress Square to City Hall, events start at 11:00 a.m. Puppet theaters, roving jugglers and magicians, family skates, laser tag, dance performances and horse drawn wagon rides are just some of the excitement. At 8:00 p.m, a huge indoor fireworks display takes place at the Civic Center. Free parking all day at the Elm Street Parking Garage and at all city meters. Contact: www.newyearsportland.com.

Room for Notes

Index by Attraction

Room for Notes

Index by Location

New Hampshire

Room for Notes

7/07